# The Fun Way
# TO
# BETTER
# BRIDGE
# PLAY

## BY HARRY LAMPERT

Published by
DEVYN PRESS, INC.
Louisville, KY

Devyn Press, Inc.
3600 Chamberlain Lane, Suite 230
Louisville, KY 40241
1-800-274-2221
FAX 502-426-2044

Printed in the U.S.A.

# TABLE OF CONTENTS

*When writing*
*a bridge book,*
*you need all the help*
*you can get.*
*I want especially to thank*
*my dear wife, Adele,*
*my favorite partner*
*...in everything.*
*Also,*
*an appreciation*
*to our daughter, Karen,*
*for her*
*valuable input.*

# Bidding
# Sets the Pace...

# Play of the Hand
## Wins the Race!

*PUFF! PUFF!*

## *PREFACE*

In bridge lessons and literature much emphasis has been placed on bidding and quite a bit less on the playing aspect of the game. I felt the need to help fill this gap for the average player.

True, getting into the right contract is important, but fulfilling it in the play is equally necessary. And what happens if you wind up in the wrong contract? The ability to limit the damage, or occasionally to convert a "sow's ear into a silk purse" reaps gratifying rewards.

We will start from ground zero and progress gradually to cover the key aspects of declarer and defensive play that come up in your games every day. We will try to provide the answers to the problems that face you on almost every hand:

How to plan the play in suit and notrump contracts; When to draw trumps and when to delay drawing trumps; When to hold up and when to win the trick; How to finesse and when to finesse and when not to; Which suit do I set up first? What suit to lead and what card to lead. We can go on and on. But we don't have to do it now. Hopefully, most of it will be covered in the pages ahead.

If you're looking for a book packed with exotic, brilliant plays that may come up once in a lifetime, this is not for you. But if you want to become a better player of the cards every day as a declarer or defender, please read on.

In preparing the hand diagrams, we have not followed the custom of bridge columns of always making South the declarer. Rather, the hands appear randomly just as in real life. This will enable the readers and their friends to replay the hands in practice sessions, giving each player a crack at a problem, as a defender or a declarer, around the table.

In indicating methods of signaling and opening leads, we've chosen those that are considered standard in current practices. As an example, we are recommending leading Ace from A K x. It eliminates the ambiguity when you lead a king, whether it's from A K x or from K Q. However, the most important thing is that you and your partner are in agreement and comfortable with whatever methods you use.

# INTRODUCTION

The bidding has proceeded on its merry way. After a series of bids and calls have been followed by three passes, the final contract bas been established. The die has been cast. It's on to the play of the hand.

If the bidding has resulted in the correct final contract, life will be easier for you as the declarer. You will try your best to fulfill the contract and perhaps garner some extra tricks along the way.

If the final contract is not ideal, you may have to struggle quite a bit harder, trying to salvage the best out of a bad situation.

Whether you are the declarer or a defender you are now at the climax of the hand: The play of the cards.

Fortunately, if one looks at bridge card play as simply as possible, it boils down to the fact that there are only three ways to win tricks:

1. High Cards
2. Long Suits
3. Trumping (Ruffing)

Believe it or not you're in the same boat as the world's greatest experts. The only ways they win tricks are also: High cards, long suits and ruffing.

## *HIGH CARDS*

If you hold an ace, you can win one trick; with an A K in a suit you can win two tricks and with A K Q you can win three tricks.

With a combination of honors such as K Q or K Q J you will lose one trick to the opponents' ace . You wind up with one trick in the first instance and two tricks in the second instance.

This principle is true in the lower ranking honors as well, with Q J 10 losing two tricks to the A K and winning one trick, or J 10 9 8 losing to the opponents' A K Q and winning one trick in the end.

The favorable location of opponents' honors vis-a-vis your honors can also result in winning tricks for your side.

High cards do win tricks.

## *LONG SUITS*

Consider this combination of cards in a suit between you and your partner, with the balance of the suit reasonably distributed between your opponents. Let us assume that you are playing in a notrump contract.

| A | | Partner | | |
|---|---|---|---|---|
| | | 7 6 5 | | |
| | Opponent | | | Opponent |
| | J 10 9 | | | 8 |
| | | You | | |
| | | A K Q 4 3 2 | | |

After you have played the ace, king, queen, the opponents are out of cards in the suit, and your deuce is now as good as your A K Q were originally. You wind up winning six tricks in the suit. So you see, long suits win tricks.

Other combinations may look something like these:

| B | | Partner | | |
|---|---|---|---|---|
| | | K 4 3 | | |
| | Opponent | | | Opponent |
| | J 10 8 | | | 9 7 |
| | | You | | |
| | | A Q 6 5 2 | | |

| C | | Partner | | |
|---|---|---|---|---|
| | | K Q J 3 2 | | |
| | Opponent | | | Opponent |
| | 10 8 7 4 | | | 9 6 |
| | | You | | |
| | | A 5 | | |

In examples B. and C. you wind up with five tricks. In all these cases, however, long suits win tricks.

## TRUMPING (or Ruffing)

When a hand is played in a suit contract, tricks can be won by trumping the opponents' high cards in any side suit in which you are void. This can be done either by the declarer or the defenders.

As a defender, for example, your partner leads an ace in a side suit and you play your singleton. On the next lead of the suit dummy plays the king, but you may win the trick by ruffing with your lowly deuce of trump!

The hand, illustrated below, will give you an idea of how ruffing can provide many tricks for the declarer.

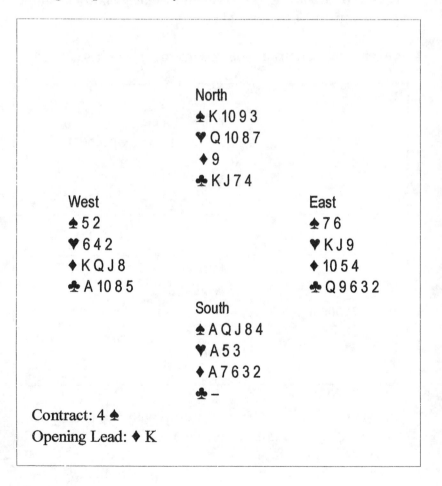

North
♠ K 10 9 3
♥ Q 10 8 7
♦ 9
♣ K J 7 4

West
♠ 5 2
♥ 6 4 2
♦ K Q J 8
♣ A 10 8 5

East
♠ 7 6
♥ K J 9
♦ 10 5 4
♣ Q 9 6 3 2

South
♠ A Q J 8 4
♥ A 5 3
♦ A 7 6 3 2
♣ –

Contract: 4 ♠
Opening Lead: ♦ K

After winning the opening lead with the ♦A, you can win nine tricks with the trump suit by alternating ruffing the opponents' high cards in diamonds in the dummy and their clubs in your hand. We call this a cross-ruff type of hand. Indeed, many tricks can be won by ruffing.

Although the premise is simple, high cards, long suits and trumping do win tricks, the methods of accomplishing good results are many.

The following chapters will try to give you a firm foundation on how to apply many of the basic techniques which will enable you to win the maximum tricks at the bridge table.

Becoming a good card player will also be an aid to you in the bidding process. You will be able to evaluate your hand not only through the point count method, but you also will have a greater awareness of the trick-taking possibilities of your hand.

♦ ♦ ♦ ♦ ♦

# HIGH CARDS

*Techniques for
winning high cards
and
developing lower honors
as tricks
in notrump and
suit contracts*

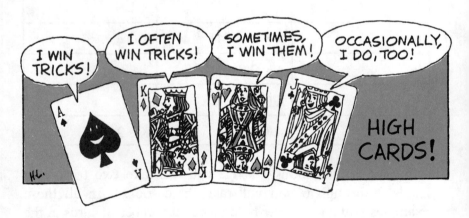

As we indicated in the introduction, HIGH CARDS WIN TRICKS. In notrump contracts it is a truism. In suit contracts it is a relative truism, provided the high cards are not trumped.

To keep our attention focused in our discussion on high cards, we will assume initially that we are in notrump contracts.

An ace can always win a trick whenever its suit is played. If a heart is played and you play the ace of hearts it will surely win the trick. Likewise, a combination of A K in the same suit will win two tricks and A K Q will win three tricks. This is true whether they are held in your hand or in combination with your partner.

| Examples | You | Dummy |
|---|---|---|
| 1. | A K | 4 3 |
| 2. | A 4 | K 3 |
| 3. | A K Q | 5 4 3 |
| 4. | A 5 3 | K Q 4 |
| 5. | A Q 5 | K 4 3 |
| 6. | A K 5 | Q 4 3 |
| 7. | A Q 5 | K 4 |
| 8. | A 5 | K Q 4 |
| 9. | A K Q 2 | J 4 3 |
| 10. | A Q J 2 | K 4 |
| 11. | A Q 4 2 | K J 2 |

In hand combinations 1 and 2 you will take two tricks. In hands 3 through 6 you will take three tricks. In all these examples you and partner hold an equal number of cards in the suit. The play of the cards presents no problem. However, in hands 7 through 11, care must be taken to ensure winning the maximum number of tricks. In this examples the number of cards in each hand of the partnership is different and the number of tricks involved is greater than the number of cards you hold in one of the hands. The order in which you play the cards is critical. The secret is: Play the high cards first from the hand that has the fewer cards.

In hand
7. Play the king first from dummy's hand.
8. Play the ace first from your hand.
9. Play the jack first from dummy.
10. Play the king first from dummy.
11. Play the king and then the jack from dummy.

♦ ♦ ♦ ♦ ♦

## CASH TRICKS IN THE RIGHT SEQUENCE

> *Dummy*
> North
> ♠ J 5 2
> ♥ J 3 2
> ♦ K Q 7 6 2
> ♣ K 3
>
> *You*
> South
> ♠ A 7 6 4
> ♥ A 8 5 4
> ♦ A J
> ♣ A 6 4

Contract: 3NT by South. Opening lead: ♣Q.

Here is a hand where all the tricks for fulfilling your contract are there for the taking. All you have to do is win them in the proper order. A slight caution: Watch out for entry problems.

9

1. How many tricks can you win?
2. With which card do you win the first trick?
3. Which suit do you play first?
4. What cards do you play first?
5. How do you reach dummy to run your long suit?

Here is the complete hand:

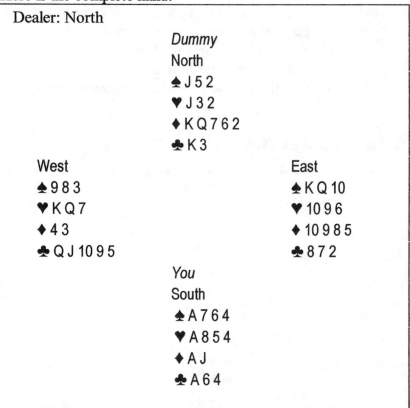

Dealer: North

Dummy
North
♠ J 5 2
♥ J 3 2
♦ K Q 7 6 2
♣ K 3

West
♠ 9 8 3
♥ K Q 7
♦ 4 3
♣ Q J 10 9 5

East
♠ K Q 10
♥ 10 9 6
♦ 10 9 8 5
♣ 8 7 2

You
South
♠ A 7 6 4
♥ A 8 5 4
♦ A J
♣ A 6 4

If you planned the play as follows you came out on top.
1. The number of tricks available are nine: one spade, one heart, five diamonds and two clubs.
2. Win the first trick with your ♣A. You'll need the ♣K later as an entry to dummy.
3&4. Play diamonds first. Play the ace followed by the jack. which unblocks the suit.
5. You reach dummy with the ♣K.

10

You now can run the balance of your diamond suit and then cash your heart and spade aces. You have nine tricks in the bag. Notice that if you had won the first trick with dummy's ♣K you would have destroyed your entry to dummy. You'd have had to overtake your ♦J to reach dummy. But that would provide only three diamond tricks as East can stop the suit with his four diamonds headed by the 10.

## DEVELOP LOWER HONORS AS WINNERS

Tricks are not always available from "the top," as presented in the previous examples. Many times you have to permit the opponents to win one or more tricks to enable you to develop winners with lower ranking honors.

Here are some examples where you hold these types of combination of honors in conjunction with your partner:

|     | You     | Dummy  |
| --- | ------- | ------ |
| A.  | K 7     | Q 6    |
| B.  | K Q     | 7 6    |
| C.  | K Q J   | 7 6 5  |
| D.  | K Q 5   | J 7 6  |
| E.  | K Q 10 3| J 7 6 2|
| F.  | Q J 10  | 7 5 2  |
| G.  | Q 7 5   | J 10 3 |
| H.  | J 10 9 3| 8 6 2  |

In hands A and B, you give up one trick to the ace and win one trick.

In hands C and D, you give up one trick to the ace and win two tricks.

In hand E, you give up a trick to the ace and win three tricks.

11

In hands F and G, you give up two tricks to the A K and win one trick.

In hand H, you give up three tricks to the A K Q and win one trick.

Let's look at the following hand and see how it works in practice.

| Dummy | | | You | |
|---|---|---|---|---|
| West | | | East | |
| ♠ K 5 3 | | | ♠ A 10 6 | |
| ♥ A 9 | | | ♥ K 7 6 | |
| ♦ J 10 9 5 | | | ♦ K Q 8 | |
| ♣ K 8 6 2 | | | ♣ A 7 5 4 | |
| Bidding: | West | North | East | South |
| | — | — | 1NT | Pass |
| | 3NT | All Pass | | |
| Opening Lead : ♥Q | | | | |

You survey your prospects of making nine tricks. You count six tricks that are available off the top, the ♠A K, ♥A K and ♣ A K.

Where can you obtain the other three tricks? By surrendering one trick to the opponents' ♦A, you will establish three tricks in the suit for yourself.

You proceed by winning the opening lead with the ♥A and immediately go about the business of establishing your three tricks in the diamond suit. Play the ♦5 from dummy and insert the ♦K from your hand. If the opponents win with the ace, you win any return and cash all your winners for nine tricks.

If the opponents hold off winning the first round of diamonds, continue with the queen, and if necessary, the jack until you've established your three diamond tricks. Upon regaining the lead cash all your nine tricks, making your contract.

The complete hand:

```
Dealer: East
                          North
                          ♠ J 7 4
                          ♥ 4 3 2
                          ♦ 7 6 4 2
                          ♣ Q J 9
        West                              East
        ♠ K 5 3                           ♠ A 10 6
        ♥ A 9                             ♥ K 7 6
        ♦ J 10 9 5                        ♦ K Q 8
        ♣ K 8 6 2                         ♣ A 7 5 4
                          South
                          ♠ Q 9 8 2
                          ♥ Q J 10 8 5
                          ♦ A 3
                          ♣ 10 3
```

Notice how important it is to establish your *lower* ranking honors *before* you cash your sure tricks with your aces and kings. If you blithely cash your aces and kings *first* you would be establishing the *opponents'* lower ranking honors for them and your contract could very well be defeated.

In the previous example hand you had to give up *one trick* to a higher ranking honor to establish your lower honors as tricks. In many instances you may have to give up *more* than one trick to establish your lower ranking honors . . . and in some cases you have to do it in more than one suit as well.

In the following hand you are again in that perennial favorite contract: 3 NT

```
Dealer: South
                          North
                          ♠ J 10 9 8
                          ♥ A 10 3
                          ♦ K 7
                          ♣ J 10 8 5

You                                        Dummy
West                                       East
♠ K Q 3 2                                  ♠ A 7 4
♥ K Q 4 2                                  ♥ J 5
♦ Q 6 4                                    ♦ J 10 3 2
♣ A 7                                      ♣ K Q 6 2

                          South
                          ♠ 6 5
                          ♥ 9 8 7 6
                          ♦ A 9 8 5
                          ♣ 9 4 3
```

| Bidding: | West | North | East | South |
|----------|------|-------|------|-------|
|          | ---  | ---   | ---  | Pass  |
|          | 1 NT | Pass  | 3 NT | All Pass |

Opening Lead; ♠J

You take stock of your combined assets and find you have six tricks available: three spade tricks and three club tricks. You have to develop three more tricks. The heart suit will account for only two tricks, after losing one honor to the ace. In order to fulfill your contract you must win a trick in diamonds. As the diamond trick will take the longest to establish, you make that task the first order of business.

After winning the opening spade lead with the ace, play a small diamond to your queen, losing to North's king. Win the likely spade return with your queen and play another diamond to dummy's 10, which loses to South's ace and establishes your ♦J as a trick.

You win any return and now set your sights on the heart suit. A small heart to dummy's jack forces out North's ace, which sets up two heart tricks, your queen and king.

The defenders must play a card which gives you the lead. *Now* you can cash all your high cards. You wind up with three spades, three clubs, two hearts and one diamond – a total of nine tricks for your contract.

♦ ♦ ♦ ♦ ♦

## DEVELOPING LOWER HONORS IN A SUIT CONTRACT

We'll now take a look at how the principle of establishing lower ranking honors works in suit contracts.

```
                        You
                        North
                        ♠ A J 9 8 7
                        ♥ Q 5
                        ♦ Q J 7
                        ♣ K 6 5
    West                                        East
    ♠ 4 2                                       ♠ 10 3
    ♥ J 10 4                                    ♥ A K 9 8
    ♦ A 10 5 2                                  ♦ 9 8 6 4
    ♣ J 8 4 3                                   ♣ Q 10 7
                        Dummy
                        South
                        ♠ K Q 6 5
                        ♥ 7 6 3 2
                        ♦ K 3
                        ♣ A 9 2
```

You arrive at a 4♠ contract after a simple auction:

| Bidding: | West | North | East | South |
|----------|------|-------|------|-------|
|          | Pass | 1 ♠   | Pass | 3 ♠*  |
|          | Pass | 4 ♠   | All Pass |   |

* Forcing raise

Opening Lead: ♥A

---

Upon viewing the dummy, you can see two sure heart losers, one sure loser in diamonds and a potential loser in clubs. As the most you can lose is three tricks to fulfill your contract, you must find a way to do away with one loser.

After the opponents win the first two tricks with the ♥A and the ♥K, you ruff the third heart lead. You first draw the opponents' trumps by playing two rounds of spades, with the ace and king.

16

Now turn your attention to the diamond suit where you want to establish *lower ranking* honors. Play the ♦K, losing to the opponents' ace, which establishes your queen and jack as the highest honors. You win any return by the defenders. (If it's a heart, you ruff it. If it's a club you win it with dummy's ace. If it's a diamond you win it with the jack.)

Let us assume the defenders lead a heart, which you ruff. Now play the ♦Q followed by the ♦J on which you *discard dummy's* ♣2. Play dummy's ♣A, small from your hand, followed by dummy's small club to your king. Dummy is now void of clubs and you can ruff your last club with one of dummy's trumps. Your club loser has now disappeared.

All you have left in your hand are trumps and you have fulfilled your contract, having lost two heart tricks and one diamond trick. Your success in this hand was a direct result of establishing *your lower ranking diamond honors.*

# CHAPTER 2

# THE FINESSE

*What it is
and what it isn't.*
♦ ♦ ♦
*Techniques for
Simple finesses,
Double finesses,
Two-way finesses,
Deep finesses
and
Ruffing finesses.*

Now that we have an idea of how to win tricks with higher ranking cards, let's look at how you can try to win tricks with *lower* ranking cards when the opponents hold *higher* ranking cards in the suit.

Doesn't it feel great to win a trick with a queen when the opponents hold the king? . . . or to win a trick with a jack when they hold a queen?   Sometimes you can win a trick with a king when they hold the ace.

The magic of this maneuver is called the "Finesse."

The FINESSE is an attempt to win tricks with lower ranking cards by taking advantage of the favorable location of higher ranking cards held by the opponents.

Let's look at this simple situation:

```
                      Dummy
                      A Q
                     ┌───────┐
   Opponent          │   N   │      Opponent
      ?              │ W   E │         ?
                     │   S   │
                     └───────┘
                      You
                      4 3
```

You would like to win two tricks with this combination. You lead from your hand and when West plays a small card, you play the queen,

If West has the king your queen wins the trick.  If East has the king he will capture your queen and win the trick.

So sometimes you win and sometimes you lose.  The finesse for the king was a 50-50 proposition.

But what was your alternative?  If you had played your ace the first time, that's the only trick you would have won.  The queen would be lost on the second trick no matter which opponent held the king.

Half a chance is certainly better than no chance!  A finesse is not a sure thing, it is a percentage play.

## THE FINESSE AGAINST THE KING

The charts below show a number of situations for simple finesses for the king.

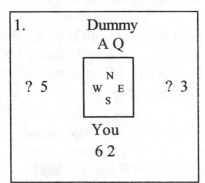

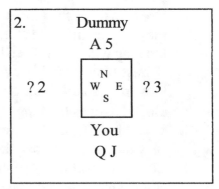

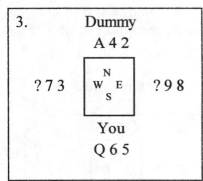

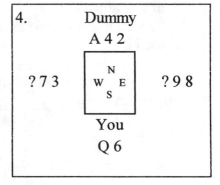

In each case you wish to win two tricks. Decide:
  A. Which defender you would like to hold the king?
     (In your mind replace the question mark with the king.)
  B. Which card would you lead from which hand?

1.  A. Hope West has the king.
    B. Lead small from South. When West plays small, play the queen from North.

2. A. Hope West has the king.
   B. Lead the queen from South; if West plays small, play small from North; if West covers with the king, win with North's ace. South's jack now becomes a trick.
3. A. Hope East has the king.
   B. Play the ace from the North hand (in the faint hope that the king will drop). Then lead small towards the queen. If East plays small, play the queen. If East plays the king, play small. Your queen is now high.
4. A. Hope East has the king.
   B. Lead small from the North hand. If East plays small, play the queen. If East plays the king, play small. Your queen is now high. Eventually you will win the ace.
   Note: This hand is different than hand Number 3. You hold only two cards in the South hand. You could not afford to play the ace first as it would bare your queen, making it susceptible to capture regardless of who held the king.

In the following charts you will try to win *three tricks* finessing for the king.

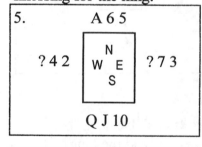

5.   A 6 5
? 4 2   N  W  E  S   ? 7 3
     Q J 10

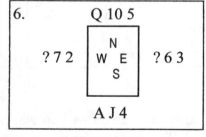

6.   Q 10 5
? 7 2   N  W  E  S   ? 6 3
     A J 4

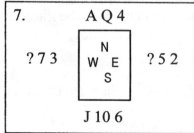

7.   A Q 4
? 7 3   N  W  E  S   ? 5 2
     J 10 6

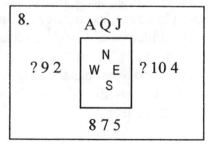

8.   A Q J
? 9 2   N  W  E  S   ? 10 4
     8 7 5

Decide:

   A.   Which defender would you like to hold the king?
       (In your mind replace the question mark with the king.)

   B.   Which card would you lead from which hand?
       Hint: Retaining the lead is an important factor in this
       series of charts. The finesse may have to be repeated in
       order to win three tricks.

5. A.   Hope West has the king.
   B.   Lead the queen from South. If West covers your queen
       with the king, win with North's ace, setting up your jack
       and 10 as tricks. If, however, West plays small, play
       small from North. Then continue the next trick with the
       jack, repeating the finesse.

6. A.   Hope East has the king.
   B.   Lead the queen from the North hand. If East does not
       cover with the king play small from the South hand. If
       it wins the trick, you have retained the lead in the North
       hand permitting you to continue the finesse on the next
       lead.

7. A.   Hope West holds the king.
   B.   Lead the jack from South. If West does not cover with
       the king you are then able to continue the finesse by
       another lead from the South hand.

8. A.   Hope that West holds the king.
   B.   Lead from South. If West plays small, insert the jack
       from North. You will note that you are now in the North
       hand. To be able to repeat the finesse you have to return
       to the South hand through another suit.

## THE FINESSE AGAINST THE ACE

All the previous examples were of simple finesses against the opponents' kings. Simple finesses can also be executed against the opponents' aces.

Here are two examples. In example 9 try to win one trick with the king. In example 10 try to win two tricks with the king and queen.

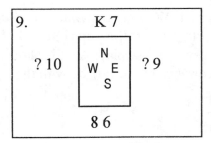

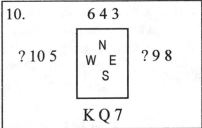

Decide:
   A. Which defender would you like to hold the ace?
   B. Which card would you lead from which hand?

9. A. Hope West has the ace.
   B. Lead small from the South hand.

If West plays the ace, naturally you would play small from the North hand. If West plays a small card you would play the king from North.

10. A. Hope East has the ace.
    B. Lead small from the North hand.

If East plays small, play South's queen. It the queen holds the trick you then have to enter the North hand through another suit and repeat the finesse again. Lead small from North and if East withholds the ace, win the trick with South's king.

## THE FINESSE AGAINST THE QUEEN

Let's drop a couple of notches lower and attempt finesses against the opponents' queen.

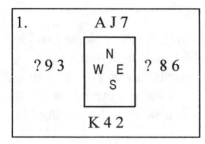

1.
```
            A J 7
                N
  ? 9 3   W       E   ? 8 6
                S
            K 4 2
```

2.
```
            J 10 3
                N
  ? 8 5   W       E   ? 9 6
                S
            A K 4
```

3.
```
            A K J
                N
  ? 4 2   W       E   ? 9 5
                S
            7 6 3
```

4.
```
            A 7 5
                N
  ? 8 3   W       E   ? 9 4
                S
            K J 6
```

A. First determine which defender you would like to hold the queen.
B. Which card would you lead from which hand?

1. A. You would like West to have the queen.
   B. You can afford to play South's king first in the faint hope of dropping an opponents' singleton queen. Then lead a small card from South's hand. If West plays small insert North's jack. If the jack wins, you've successfully executed the finesse.

2. A. You would like East to have the queen.
   B. The finesse is executed by leading the jack from the North hand. If East plays a small card, you play small

from South. If your wishes are realized and East holds the queen the finesse is successful. Naturally, if East had covered the jack with the queen, you would have won it with the king, setting up North's 10 as a winner.

Note: If you have sufficient entries in the North hand it is often wise to cash one of South's high honors first in the slight hope that the opponents' queen is a singleton. If the queen does not fall, North is entered through another suit, and the finesse is than taken by leading the jack as indicated before.

3. A.   You would want West to hold the queen.
   B.   The finesse is executed by leading from the South hand. If West plays low insert the jack, hopefully winning the finesse. (Again, if sufficient entries permit, first play North's king in the rare hope of dropping a singleton queen. If it drops, the finesse is unnecessary. If not, as usually happens, reach the South hand in another suit and take the finesse as indicated above.)

4. A.   East should hold the queen.
   B.   Execute the finesse by leading the ace from the North hand. If the queen does not fall singleton, lead again from the North hand and finesse with South's jack. Note that technically this example is similar to Hand 1. Just the ace, king and directions have been changed. We've included it to indicate that simple finesses can take many forms. They may look a little different, but they are basically the same.

♦ ♦ ♦ ♦ ♦

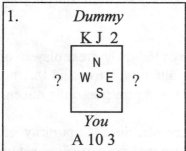

1. *Dummy*
   K J 2
   ? W E ?
   *You*
   A 10 3

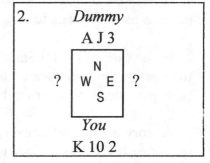

2. *Dummy*
   A J 3
   ? W E ?
   *You*
   K 10 2

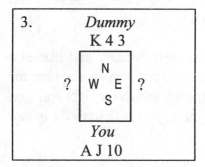

3. *Dummy*
   K 4 3
   ? W E ?
   *You*
   A J 10

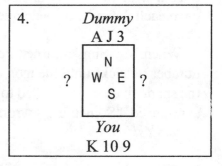

4. *Dummy*
   A J 3
   ? W E ?
   *You*
   K 10 9

Here again you're finessing for the queen. But this time you have a combination of cards that permit you to finesse either way. It makes no difference which opponent holds the queen.

If you have your Ouija board working for you, perhaps you can guess the right way. A more practical way is to look for signs in the bidding or play that would tend to indicate which defender holds the queen.

If you have reason to believe East has the queen, play your high honor (ace or king) from the North hand and then finesse against East's hoped-for queen.

If your perception is that West holds the queen, then your procedure is the reverse. Play your high honor first from the South hand and take your finesses through West.

If you have no guidelines as to the location of the queen, your guess is as good as mine.

In the case of P. Hal Sims, one of the truly great players of the thirties, things appeared to be different. It is said that his table presence was so great that he never misguessed a queen.

A story is told that one day when Mr. Sims temporarily left the room, his friends decided to play a trick on him. They set up a hand with a two-way finesse situation in the spade suit, and gave each defender a spade queen.

When Mr. Sims returned he became declarer and played a number of tricks until the moment of truth arrived, the time for the spade finesse. He looked to the left and to the right and then announced, "Something's wrong here, you *both* have the *queen of spades!*"

Although we normal mortals have to rely on judgment and luck in these situations, a little psychological ploy is available to us in hands such as Numbers 3 and 4 where we hold sufficient back-up cards.

In Hand 3, lead the jack from South. If West covers with the queen your problem is solved. If West doesn't cover, go up with the king and then lead small from North and finesse with the 10.

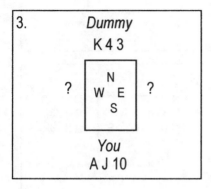

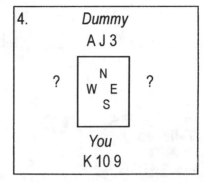

Likewise in Hand 4, lead the jack from dummy. If it is not covered with the queen, hop up with your king and then lead South's 10 for a finesse against West's hoped-for queen.

This ploy is based upon players' habit of covering an honor with an honor (or making a pronounced pause for thought, revealing the location of the queen). Remember, it is unethical "to pause and think as if you have the queen," when you, in fact, do not.

## IS IT OR IS IT NOT A FINESSE?

As a note of caution, we'd like you to be able to differentiate between what may *appear* to be a finesse situation and what is *truly* a finesse situation.

**A.**

```
          J 10 4
          ┌─────┐
          │  N  │
9 6 5     │W   E│   Q 8 7 2
          │  S  │
          └─────┘
          A K 3
```
*Finesse*

**B.**

```
          J 4 3
          ┌─────┐
          │  N  │
9 6 5     │W   E│   Q 8 7 2
          │  S  │
          └─────┘
          A K 10
```
*Finesse*

**C.**

```
          J 4 3
          ┌─────┐
          │  N  │
10 9 6    │W   E│   Q 8 7 2
          │  S  │
          └─────┘
          A K 5
```
No Finesse !

THIS IS **NO** FINESSE!

If the West hand holds the queen plus two or more cards, you cannot win three tricks in any of the three examples shown. Therefore, to make a successful finesse you have to assume that East holds the queen.

In diagrams A and B, when the jack is led from the North hand and it is covered by East's queen, South can win it with the king and the 10 is now set up as the third trick.

However, in diagram C, if the jack is led from North and is covered by East's queen, South can win it with the king but the *opponents'* 10 and adjacent cards are set up as *their* tricks.

Diagram C is not a finesse. When a jack is unaccompanied by either the ace or king in the same hand it is not a simple finesse for the queen unless the combined hands also contain the 10.

In diagram C, where a finesse is not possible, the only hope for three tricks is for one of the opponents to hold a doubleton queen.

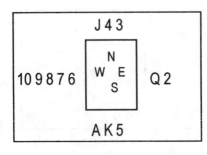 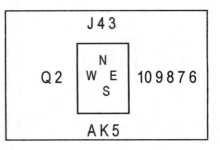

It make no difference which opponent holds the queen. The correct play is AK. If the queen falls as in the diagrams above, your jack becomes the third trick.

### THE DOUBLE FINESSE

All the finesses discussed to this point were based upon *one* key card missing ... either the ace, king or queen. We will now look into the double-finesse, where two key cards are missing.

In each of these examples you are trying to win two tricks, although two key cards are missing. All prior finesses, with *one* key card missing, had a 50 percent chance of winning, depending upon the location of the missing honor.

In examples 1A & 1B and 2A & 2B, your chances of success to win two tricks are *75 percent*.

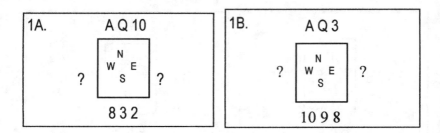

In hands 1A & 1B you are missing the king and the jack.

In 1A the proper procedure is to lead a small card from the South hand. When a small card is played by West, insert North's 10. If it loses to the jack obtain the lead in South and finesse again with the queen. Three out of four times you should win, because these are the four possible distributions of the opponents' honors:

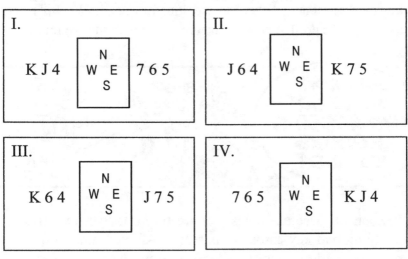

In the first circumstance, with both honors in the West hand, you will win *all three tricks* by finessing first with the ten, then returning to the South hand in another suit, leading small and finessing with the queen.

In the second case, the finesse of the 10 loses to East's king, setting up your ace and queen as winners.

In the third case, your 10 finesse loses to the jack. Upon obtaining the lead again in South, you lead small and successfully finesse against West's king.

Only in the fourth case would your finesses lose to both the jack and the king in the East hand. But you would have lost anyway if you had not finessed.

Try to recognize that example 1B is basically the same as example 1A. In 1A all honors are concentrated in one hand, North. In 1B the honors are divided between the two hands. Additional contiguous cards are necessary to make the finesses effective. The South hand is buttressed by the 9 and 8.

The proper initial play therefore would be the 10 from the South hand. If it is not covered by West, simply let it ride for the finesse.

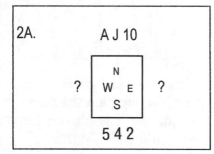

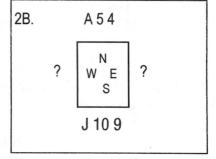

In hands 2A & 2B you are missing the king and queen.

Lead from the South hand and finesse with the jack. If it loses to an honor in the East hand, upon regaining the lead, play from South and finesse again.

Statistically you should be successful three out of four times. Naturally, if an honor is ever played by the West hand, you should cover it with North's ace. That would automatically set up one of your lower honors as a trick.

33

Here are the possible divisions of the opponents' honors.

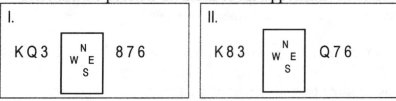

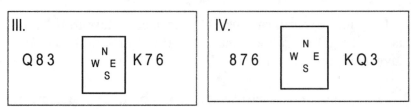

By finessing you win in the first three layouts and lose in the fourth, a 75 percent chance of success.

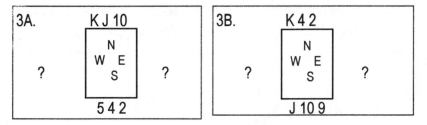

In hands 3A & 3B you are missing the ace and queen.

As the ace must be lost in any event, the situation should be treated as a simple finesse for the queen. The chance for success is therefore a 50 percent proposition.

Your hope in these examples is for West to have the queen. Lead from the South hand finessing with the jack if a small card is played from the West hand.

1. If it loses to East's ace, regain the lead again in the South hand and repeat the finesse.

2. If the first finesse is successful and wins the trick, return to the South hand in another suit in hand 3A and repeat the finesse. In 3B you can repeat it immediately.

3.  If West rises with the ace, play small from the North
    hand. Reenter the South hand upon regaining the lead,
    and repeat the finesse against West's queen.

These are the likely divisions of opponents' honors that will
result in a successful finesse:

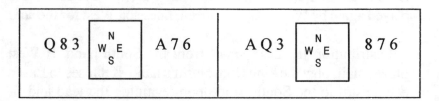

In hands 4A and 4B you are missing the ace and the jack.

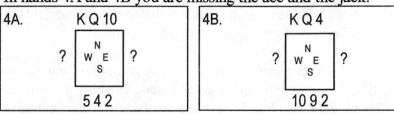

These are the four possible distributions of the opponents'
honors.

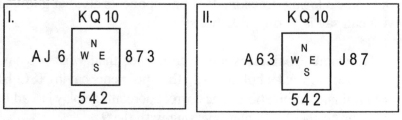

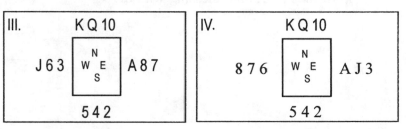

Distribution I presents no problems as long as you lead from the South hand. Distribution IV has no hope no matter how you play it. That leaves II and III as the pertinent distributions.

Distribution II: Lead small from the South hand. If West plays small, play North's king. If it wins, return to the South hand in another suit. Lead toward the queen; if a small card is played again by West, play the queen, finessing West for the ace.

Distribution III: Lead small from the South hand. If West plays small, play the king from North's hand. If it loses to East's ace, return to the South hand upon regaining the lead and finesse the 10 against West's hoped for ace.

Your success in this maneuver will depend a great deal upon the ability and sophistication of your opponents.

The defender in the East seat, though holding the ace, can refrain from winning the trick and smoothly play a small card. This may lull you into believing West has the ace. On the next finesse you may then make the correct percentage play (as indicated in distribution II above) of the queen, but it would turn out to be a losing decision. If your opponents are that good, all you can say is, "congratulations!"

Occasionally, finesses are even deeper than what we have discussed. An A J 9 holding with the opponents having K Q 10, is a familiar combination. The correct percentage play is leading small up to the A J 9, and finessing with the 9.

◆ ◆ ◆ ◆ ◆

36

Here is a fun hand encompassing some of the finesses we discussed. Take every finesse in sight and see how many tricks you can win. Watch your communications so that you can repeat successful finesses.

```
Dealer: North
                        North
                        ♠ 8 6 4
                        ♥ A Q J
                        ♦ J 10 9 3
                        ♣ A Q 10

        West                        East
        ♠ 9 5                       ♠ Q 10 7 3
        ♥ K 10 9 6 3                ♥ 8 5 4
        ♦ 5 4                       ♦ K 8 6
        ♣ K J 9 7                   ♣ 5 3 2

                        South
                        ♠ A K J 2
                        ♥ 7 2
                        ♦ A Q 7 2
                        ♣ 8 6 4
```

| Bidding: | West | North | East | South |
|----------|------|-------|------|-------|
|          | ---  | 1♦    | Pass | 1♠    |
|          | Pass | 1 NT  | Pass | 3♦    |
|          | Pass | 3 NT  |      | All Pass |

Opening Lead:  ♠3

If you did everything right, you wound up with 13 tricks. If you made less, try and try again until you get it right!

♦ ♦ ♦ ♦ ♦

All the finesse techniques described so far are possible in both trump and notrump contracts. The ruffing finesse is available for use in a side suit only in a trump contract.

The idea is to attempt to set up lower ranking honors by ruffing the opponents' higher honor. Even if the opponents' honor is not well placed, the discard of a loser on a loser often makes the maneuver effective.

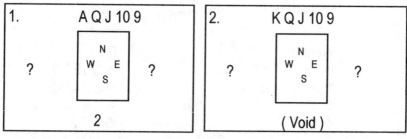

The diagrams above are of side suits in a trump contract.

1. Lead South's singleton to North's ace. Next, lead the queen. If East covers with the king, ruff it. The J 10 9 are now established as winners. If the king is not played, discard a loser in another suit.

2. Lead the king from North. If East plays the ace, ruff it. The Q J 10 9 are established as winners. If the ace is not played, discard a loser in another suit.

In both cases, if the opponents' high honor is well-placed, you lose no tricks and you've set up your winners as well. If the defenders' key honors are in the wrong hand, you will lose a trick but you will be discarding a loser and setting up winners at the same time.

Here is an example of how the ruffing finesse can work in an actual hand:

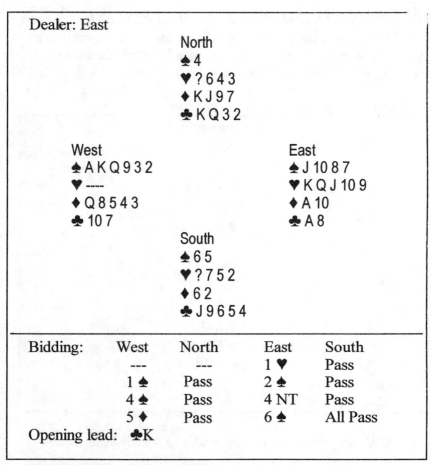

Dealer: East

**North**
- ♠ 4
- ♥ ? 6 4 3
- ♦ K J 9 7
- ♣ K Q 3 2

**West**
- ♠ A K Q 9 3 2
- ♥ ----
- ♦ Q 8 5 4 3
- ♣ 10 7

**East**
- ♠ J 10 8 7
- ♥ K Q J 10 9
- ♦ A 10
- ♣ A 8

**South**
- ♠ 6 5
- ♥ ? 7 5 2
- ♦ 6 2
- ♣ J 9 6 5 4

| Bidding: | West | North | East | South |
|---|---|---|---|---|
| | --- | --- | 1 ♥ | Pass |
| | 1 ♠ | Pass | 2 ♠ | Pass |
| | 4 ♠ | Pass | 4 NT | Pass |
| | 5 ♦ | Pass | 6 ♠ | All Pass |
| Opening lead: ♣K | | | | |

The ♣A wins, trumps are drawn, winning the second round in dummy. The ♥K is led.

A. If South covers with the ace, you ruff it. You now enter dummy with the ♦A and play your established heart winners, discarding a club and three diamond losers. You lose one diamond at the end.

B. If the ♥K is not covered, discard your club loser. If North wins with the ♥A, you now can ruff the likely ♣Q return. Enter dummy with the ♦A. Run the heart winners discarding your four diamond losers.

39

# CHOOSING THE MOST EFFECTIVE FINESSE

Ofttimes you have a number of finesses available within one hand. You may have to make a choice between finesses or the sequence in which you take them.

Let's look at this hand:

| | |
|---|---|
| | *Dummy* |
| | North |
| | ♠ A K |
| | ♥ 8 6 5 4 |
| | ♦ K 8 7 2 |
| | ♣ 8 6 2 |
| | |
| | *You* |
| | South |
| | ♠ 3 2 |
| | ♥ A Q J |
| | ♦ A J 3 |
| | ♣ K J 10 4 3 |
| Contract   3 NT | |
| Opening Lead:  ♠Q | |

As West makes the opening lead you survey your assets.

1. How many tricks do you have available without relinquishing the lead?
2. How can you obtain the additional tricks to fulfill your contract?
3. Are there any finesses possible?
   How many?
4. Which suit gives the best opportunity to get all the tricks you need?

You have five tricks available "off the top." Two spades, one heart, and two diamonds. You need four more tricks for your contract. You have three suits and three finesse possibilities staring you in the face. Which do you take?

40

If everything goes perfectly in either hearts or diamonds, you pick up only three extra tricks in hearts or two extra tricks in diamonds. Neither is enough for your contract. If your finesse works in clubs you can pick up four additional tricks.

So that's your best bet for that contract.

After winning the opening lead with the ♠K, lead a small club. When East plays small, finesse for the queen with the ♣10. If it wins, return to dummy with the ♦K and finesse again for East's hoped-for queen. If the finesse is successful, but loses to the ace, win the expected spade return and take the finesse again.

This is the complete hand:

| Dealer: South | | North | |
|---|---|---|---|
| | | ♠ A K | |
| | | ♥ 8 6 5 4 | |
| | | ♦ K 8 7 2 | |
| | | ♣ 8 6 2 | |
| **West** | | | **East** |
| ♠ Q J 9 8 | | | ♠ 10 7 6 5 4 |
| ♥ K 10 9 7 | | | ♥ 3 2 |
| ♦ Q 10 9 | | | ♦ 6 5 4 |
| ♣ A 7 | | | ♣ Q 9 5 |
| | | **South** | |
| | | ♠ 3 2 | |
| | | ♥ A Q J | |
| | | ♦ A J 3 | |
| | | ♣ K J 10 4 3 | |

| Bidding: | West | North | East | South |
|---|---|---|---|---|
| | ---- | ---- | ---- | 1 NT |
| | Pass | 3 NT | All Pass | |
| Contract: | 3 NT | | | |
| Opening lead: | ♠Q | | | |

## WHAT'S YOUR BEST CHANCE?

In bridge, as in life, things are not often certain. We have to make choices of plays that give us the best chance of success.

In our discussions of the finesse, we become aware that it is a percentage play. The most common finesses we've covered are 50 percent and 75 percent propositions. Others of a deeper nature go down to ranges of 40 and 25 percent.

In deciding your course of action you often have to consider your probabilities of success.

Let us examine this hand.

| *Dummy* | *You* |
|---------|-------|
| ♠ K 5 4 | ♠ A 6 2 |
| ♥ 4 3 | ♥ K J 7 |
| ♦ 8 6 4 | ♦ A J 10 3 2 |
| ♣ K Q 8 6 5 | ♣ A 2 |

Contract: 3 NT
Opening Lead: ♠Q

1. How many tricks do you have available "off the top?"
2. Where are additional tricks available?
3. Which suit gives you the best percentage chance of success?
4. How do you proceed?

With six tricks available off the top, two spades, one diamond and three clubs, you look for the best place to obtain the three additional tricks necessary for your contract.

A casual look would indicate that the club and diamond suits appear to be likely candidates.

The five-card club suit could supply two additional tricks if the opponents' holdings were divided 3-3 (approximately a 36 percent chance). But that is only two tricks and you need three.

The diamond suit, where a double-finesse is possible, can deliver three additional tricks if the finesse is successful. (This double-finesse, as we had discussed earlier, has a 75 percent chance of success.)

Here is the complete hand:

```
Dealer: West           North
                       ♠ 8 3
                       ♥ 10 9 6 5
                       ♦ Q 7 5
                       ♣ J 10 9 7

        West                              East
        ♠ K 5 4                           ♠ A 6 2
        ♥ 4 3                             ♥ K J 7
        ♦ 8 6 4                           ♦ A J 10 3 2
        ♣ K Q 8 6 5                       ♣ A 2
                       South
                       ♠ Q J 10 9 7
                       ♥ A Q 8 2
                       ♦ K 9
                       ♣ 4 3
```

| Bidding: | West | North | East | South |
|----------|------|-------|------|-------|
|          | Pass | Pass  | 1 NT | Pass  |
|          | 2 NT | Pass  | 3 NT | All Pass |

Opening Lead: ♠Q

43

The play might go something like this:

Win the opening lead with the ♠K in dummy. Lead a small diamond and finesse with the 10, if a small card is played by North. It loses to South's king. A spade is returned to your ace.

You now have to return to dummy with the club suit in order to take the second diamond finesse. But you want to cash at least three club tricks, so you have to play your ♣A first to unblock the suit, and then small to dummy's ♣Q. Play the ♣K, discarding a small spade from your hand.

Now you lead a diamond from dummy intending to finesse again if North plays small. In this hand the finesse works and you run the balance of the suit, which provides all the tricks you need for your contract.

♦ ♦ ♦ ♦ ♦

The charts on the following page are a recap of the most prevalent finesses you will encounter.

# CHART OF FAMILIAR FINESSES

## SIMPLE FINESSES

### FOR THE ACE

| K X | K Q X |
|-----|-------|
| N<br>W  E<br>S | N<br>W  E<br>S |
| X X | X X X |

### FOR THE KING

| A Q | A X |
|-----|-----|
| N<br>W  E<br>S | N<br>W  E<br>S |
| X X | Q J |

| A Q J | A X X |
|-------|-------|
| N<br>W  E<br>S | N<br>W  E<br>S |
| X X X | Q J 10 |

| A X X | A X X |
|-------|-------|
| N<br>W  E<br>S | N<br>W  E<br>S |
| Q X X | Q X |

### FOR THE QUEEN

| A K J | A K X |
|-------|-------|
| N<br>W  E<br>S | N<br>W  E<br>S |
| X X X | J 10 X |

| A J X | K J X |
|-------|-------|
| N<br>W  E<br>S | N<br>W  E<br>S |
| K X X | A X X |

## DOUBLE FINESSES

| K J 10 | A J 10 |
|--------|--------|
| N<br>W  E<br>S | N<br>W  E<br>S |
| X X X | X X X |

| A Q 10 | K Q 10 |
|--------|--------|
| N<br>W  E<br>S | N<br>W  E<br>S |
| X X X | X X X |

## TWO-WAY FINESSES

| A J X | A J 10 |
|-------|--------|
| N<br>W  E<br>S | N<br>W  E<br>S |
| K 10 X | K X X |

## RUFFING FINESSES IN SUIT CONTRACTS

| A Q J 10 | K Q J 10 |
|----------|----------|
| N<br>W  E<br>S | N<br>W  E<br>S |
| X | VOID |

## DEEP FINESSES

| A J 9 | A J X |
|-------|-------|
| N<br>W  E<br>S | N<br>W  E<br>S |
| X X X | 9 8 X |

# LONG SUITS

*Techniques for
taking full advantage
of this valuable asset
in notrump
and suit contracts.*

♦ ♦ ♦ ♦

*How to give and gain tricks.*

♦ ♦ ♦ ♦

*Maintaining controls
and entries.*

Long suits are an excellent source of winning tricks in both suit and notrump contracts. Our bidding system recognizes their worth by providing additional points on evaluating hands which contain long suits.

Proper techniques are necessary to obtain the full value of this important asset. A common error by players can be avoided by the simple procedure of playing the *high cards first* from the hand containing *the fewer cards*.

When, in one of my classes, I used an illustration on a chart similar to the one on the following page, one of my students succinctly said, "On, you mean get the little fat fellow out of the way first!" She said it so well that I've been using that expression ever since to describe this principle.

**Hand 1.** First play the king, followed by the queen, then a small card to South's ace. You are now in the proper hand to run the balance of the tricks in the suit. Notice what would have happened if you first had led the ace from the South hand, followed by the deuce to North's king and then the queen. You would now be in the North hand with no more cards in the suit available to play. If you had no other way to reach the South hand the three good tricks there would go to waste.

**Hand 2.** The proper sequence of plays is ace, followed by the queen and then a small card to South's king ro run the balance of the suit.

**Hand 3.** Play the king from the North hand, then the trey to South's ace to run a total of five tricks.

The same principle applies when you have to relinquish one or more tricks to the opponents before you can set up the balance of tricks as winners.

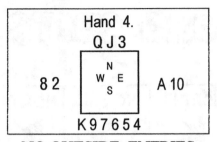

Hand 4.
Q J 3

8 2

N
W   E
S

A 10

K 9 7 6 5 4

NO OUTSIDE ENTRIES
IN SOUTH'S HAND

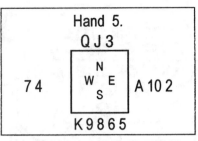

Hand 5.
Q J 3

7 4

N
W   E
S

A 10 2

K 9 8 6 5

ONE OUTSIDE ENTRY
IN SOUTH'S HAND

### Hand 4.

*Correct Play*: If the queen is played first from the North hand followed by the jack, East has to win the ace. Later, South's hand can be entered by playing North's trey to South's king to run the balance of the suit.

*Incorrect Play:* If the king is led from the South hand, and North follows with the trey, East can win with his ace at any time. With no outside entry to South's hand, the suit is limited to two tricks.

### Hand 5.

*Correct Play:* Lead the queen from the North hand, followed by the jack and then the trey, East holding up the ace to the third round. In this case South has one outside entry. Upon re-gaining the lead, South can be reached with its outside entry to run the balance of the long suit — a total of four tricks.

*Incorrect Play:* Lead the king from South hand. East wins the trick with the ace. East leads the suit which removes the outside entry from South's hand. Result: The long suit is limited to two tricks, the queen and jack in the North hand.

Let's see how the principle works in this hand:

```
Dealer: North
                            North
                            ♠ 8 6
                            ♥ A 9 5
                            ♦ K 7 6 3 2
                            ♣ J 9 8
        West                                East
        ♠ 9 5                               ♠ Q J 10 3 2
        ♥ Q J 10 8 2                        ♥ 7 4 3
        ♦ 5 4                               ♦ A 10 9
        ♣ K Q 3 2                           ♣ 6 4
                            South
                            ♠ A K 7 4
                            ♥ K 6
                            ♦ Q J 8
                            ♣ A 10 7 5
```

| Bidding: | West | North | East | South |
|----------|------|-------|------|-------|
|          | —    | Pass  | Pass | 1 NT  |
|          | Pass | 2 NT  | Pass | 3 NT  |
|          | All Pass |   |      |       |

Opening Lead: ♥Q

1. How many tricks do you have available before you relinquish the lead?
2. Where can you obtain the extra tricks you need for your contract?
3. In which hand do you take the opening lead?
4. What card do you play to the second trick?.

You have five tricks off the top. You need four more for your contract. No extra tricks are possible in spades and hearts. The club suit, even if everything lay perfectly, can deliver only two additional tricks. The diamond suit, with a reasonable distribution, can deliver four tricks by losing one trick to the opponents' ace.

You plan the play with that strategy in mind. Win the first trick with the heart king, and immediately go after the diamond suit. (You may need dummy's ace later as an entry to run the diamond suit.)

Carefully lead the queen from your hand *first*, and then the jack and a third diamond until a defender wins the ace. The ♥A is still available as an entry to dummy to run the balance of the diamond suit, assuring the fulfillment of your contract.

### SOW A LITTLE, REAP A LOT

Unless you're in a grand slam contract, it is often advisable and necessary to give up tricks to the opponents in order to set up tricks in long suits.

If you can set up a six-card suit by relinquishing one trick to the opposition, you wind up with a net gain of five tricks. If it requires a loss of two tricks your net gain is four tricks.

Similarly, it works with five and four card suits as well. If your contract can afford these losses, it is worthwhile.

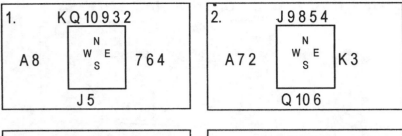

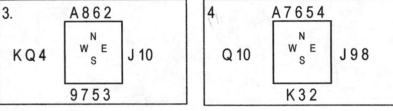

**Example 1:** Lead South's jack. Continue the suit until the opponents play the ace. The suit is set up for five tricks.

**Example 2:** Lead South's queen, which East's king wins. Upon regaining the lead, lead South's 10 and continue until West wins with the ace. Three tricks have been established for the suit.

**Example 3:** Play small from South and from North, allowing opponents to win the trick. Win any return and then play the ace and another card, which loses to West's king. You have established one extra winner in the suit.

**Example 4:** Play South's king, and then play small from both hands, giving up a trick to the opponents. Win any return and then play to North's ace and run the balance of the suit. The suit delivers a total of four tricks. Notice how the ace was retained as an entry to enable you to reach the North hand to run the suit. This brings us to the next topic.

There are often circumstances where you want to set up a suit in either your own or dummy's hand. The stumbling block is that you have no entries other than *within* the suit itself.

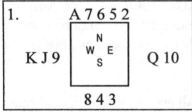

Try to win three tricks.

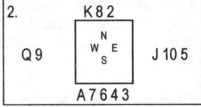

Try to win four tricks.

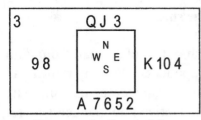

Try to win four tricks.

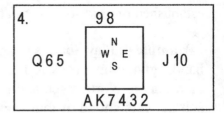

Try to win five tricks.

1. In this example you dare not play North's ace until the third round. It is your only entry to the suit. The proper play, therefore, is first to relinquish two tricks in the suit, hoping for a 3-2 split in the opponents' hands. Mechanically it could

54

go something like this: Lead small from the South hand, West plays the 9, small from North, East winning with the 10. You regain the lead in another suit. Play the key suit again, small cards from each hand, permitting either opponent to win the trick. Upon obtaining the lead again, you *play to the ace* and continue the suit, winning two more tricks with North's 7 and 6.

2. Play small from both hands, permitting the opponents to win their trick. Upon regaining the lead, play North's king, small from South, followed by small to South's ace. If the suit breaks as in the diagram, continue to play South's 7 and 6. You wind up with four tricks.

3. You can lead from either hand. If you lead the queen from North's hand and East covers it with the king, you must play *small*, allowing the opponents to win the trick. Upon regaining the lead you run the suit by winning the next trick with the jack, followed by the ace, 7 and 6. That gives you your four tricks. (If East ducks the first play of the queen, you play small, and then play small again when your jack is covered on the second round. You've retained your ace as an entry to run the suit.)

4. You must play small from both hands, surrendering the first trick. When you regain the lead play South's king, followed by the ace and the balance of the suit to give you five tricks.

Let's see how these theories work in practice.

| *Dummy* | *You* |
|---|---|
| West | East |
| ♠ 10 6 5 | ♠ A K 7 |
| ♥ Q 7 | ♥ A 10 6 |
| ♦ A K 8 6 2 | ♦ 9 7 5 |
| ♣ 7 5 3 | ♣ A K 9 6 |

Contract: 3NT
Opening Lead: ♥ 4

1. How many tricks do you have off the top?
2  Where's your best chance of getting the extra tricks you need for your contract?
3. How do you proceed?

The complete hand:

Dealer: North:

North
♠ Q J 9 8
♥ K J 2
♦ 10 4
♣ 10 8 4 2

West
♠ 10 6 5
♥ Q 7
♦ A K 8 6 2
♣ 7 5 3

East
♠ A K 7
♥ A 10 6
♦ 9 7 5
♣ A K 9 6

South
♠ 4 3 2
♥ 9 8 5 4 3
♦ Q J 3
♣ Q J

| Bidding: | West | North | East | South |
|---|---|---|---|---|
| | --- | Pass | 1 NT | Pass |
| | 3 NT | All Pass | | |

Opening Lead:  ♥4

1. You have seven tricks available off the top.
2. Diamonds are a girl's or a guy's best friend this time.

3. Play small from dummy on the opening heart lead. When East plays the jack, you win with your ace. (This guarantees a second stopper in the suit.) You go after diamonds for the extra tricks you need. There are no entries to dummy outside the diamond suit. Play small to dummy's king and then a small card to your 9, giving the trick to the defenders. If the defenders continue the heart suit, you can win the second lead with your 10. You lead your last diamond to dummy's ace allowing you to run the balance of the suit. You wind up with 10 tricks, an overtrick for your 3NT contract.

Let's take a crack at this hand.

*You*
North
♠ A 10 9
♥ A K 8
♦ A J 8 6 2
♣ J 10

*Dummy*
South
♠ Q 6
♥ 6 4 2
♦ 4 3
♣ A K 7 6 5 4

Contract: 3NT
Opening Lead: ♥Q

Plan the play of the hand:
1. How many immediate winners do you have?
2. Where can you get the balance of the tricks you require?

1. Okay! You've got six winners off the top.
2. Looks like the club suit can deliver the extra three tricks you need. You win the first heart trick and play the ♣J. Your friendly opponent covers it with the queen. What card do you play from dummy? Why?

The complete hand:

Dealer: West

```
                           You
                           North
                           ♠ A 10 9
                           ♥ A K 8
                           ♦ A J 8 6 2
                           ♣ J 10

West                                        East
♠ K J 7 4 3 2                               ♠ 8 5
♥ 7 5                                       ♥ Q J 10 9 3
♦ 9 7 5                                     ♦ K Q 10
♣ 8 3                                       ♣ Q 9 2

                           Dummy
                           South
                           ♠ Q 6
                           ♥ 6 4 2
                           ♦ 4 3
                           ♣ A K 7 6 5 4
```

| Bidding: | West | North | East | South |
|----------|------|-------|------|-------|
|          | Pass | 1 NT  | Pass | 3 NT  |
|          | All Pass |   |      |       |

Opening Lead: ♥Q

The key to the hand is: beware of opponents bearing gifts. Your goal is to bring in five tricks in the club suit. You have no entry into dummy's hand other than in the club suit.

Although the defender's club queen sets up your 10, you cannot afford to win the trick in dummy. You must duck the trick to maintain communications in the club suit. Win any return and then play your ♣10 to dummy's king. When the defenders' holding in clubs breaks 3-2, you can run the suit for your contract.

## FOUR CARD SUITS WORK TOO

In discussing long suits we usually speak about those of five or more cards. Even suits of four cards can establish an extra winner as illustrated by the hand below.

```
                    North
                    ♠ A J 7 4
                    ♥ 10 3 2
                    ♦ Q J 9 7
                    ♣ Q 10

West                                East
You                                 Dummy
♠ K 8                               ♠ Q 9 6
♥ A Q J 9 6                         ♥ K 8 7 5
♦ 8 6                               ♦ A K
♣ A 8 5 4                           ♣ 9 7 6 3

                    South
                    ♠ 10 5 3 2
                    ♥ 4
                    ♦ 10 5 4 3 2
                    ♣ K J 2
```

| Bidding: | West | North | East | South |
|---|---|---|---|---|
| | — | — | — | Pass |
| | 1♥ | Pass | 3♥ | Pass |
| | 4♥ | All Pass | | |

Opening Lead: ♦Q

Your 4♥ contract is reached easily. Counting your losers, you have one spade loser and three possible club losers. Counting winners, you have five hearts, two diamonds and one club, giving you eight tricks. You can establish your ninth trick by forcing out the ♠A. Where will your tenth trick come from? Your four-card club suit may very well supply the answer. With eight cards between you and partner, you can establish your fourth club as a trick. All you need is a normal 3-2 split in the defenders' hands.

The play could go something like this:

After winning the opening diamond lead, draw the opponents' trumps in three rounds, ending in dummy. Lead a small spade to your king, which loses to the ace. Win the likely diamond lead, cash the ♠Q and ruff the last spade in your hand. Play a small club from each hand, losing the trick to a defender. Duck the next club lead again and win the next club with the ace, setting up the fourth club as a trick. You've made your contract winning five hearts, two diamonds, one spade and two clubs.

♦ ♦ ♦ ♦ ♦

# CHAPTER 4

# DECLARER PLAY
# IN SUIT CONTRACTS

*Planning the play
of the hand.*

♦ ♦ ♦♦

*How to count losers
and winners.*

♦ ♦ ♦ ♦

*How to get rid of losers,
using the techniques
we've been discussing:
Ruffing,
Finessing,
Setting Up
Winners and Long Suits
for discards.*

How often have you seen declarers whiz through the first few tricks like greased lightning and then stew over the rest of the hand?

I guess they're trying to figure out how to undo all the damage they created in the beginning. They usually find out it's a case of locking the hangar after the helicopter's been stolen.

Unfortunately, after they've played hastily to the first trick, the damage done often cannot be rectified.

### THE KEY TO GOOD DECLARER PLAY IS PLANNING

You have to get yourself into a ritual of planning before dummy's card is played to the first trick. I make it a rule *never to permit anybody else*, not even dummy, to play dummy's first card, even if it's a singleton. I want the opportunity to plan the hand.

The time spent up front in planning pays dividends for all players at the table. It usually results in time saved through efficient declarer play and avoidance of procrastination.

To see how the planning process works, let's look at this hand through the eyes and mind of the declarer.

---

*Declarer*

North

♠ K Q 5
♥ K J 9 7 4
♦ A 8 3
♣ 10 8

*Dummy*

South

♠ A 7 4 3
♥ A 3 2
♦ K 2
♣ J 7 4 3

Contract: 4♥
Opening Lead: ♣A

---

### 1. *HOW DO I COUNT LOSERS?*

My contract is 4♥, so I can afford only three losers. Let's see how many sure losers and how many possible losers I have.

In clubs I have two sure losers. In diamonds, I have the ace and king, but I have a third diamond, that's one possible loser. In trumps I have a possible loser to the queen. I have no spade losers, with the ace, king, queen in the combined hands. This adds up to four losers: two sure losers plus two possible losers.

### 2. *WHAT CAN I DO ABOUT MY POSSIBLE LOSERS?*

In diamonds, dummy has a doubleton, so I can ruff my loser there. In hearts, if the queen is favorably located in the West hand I can try a finesse.

## 3. *WHICH SUIT DO I PLAY FIRST?*

Do I draw trumps first or play to ruff my diamond loser? I cannot afford to draw all the opponents' trumps first, because I need a trump in dummy to ruff my diamond loser.

A simple way to play the hand would be to cash the ♦K and ♦A and ruff my third diamond in dummy. Now I can try the trump finesse. I cash dummy's ♥A, and then lead toward my ♥K J and finesse against West's possible queen. If it succeeds, I've made an overtrick. If not, I've made 10 tricks, my contract.

The complete hand:

| Dealer: North | North | |
|---|---|---|
| | ♠ K Q 5 | |
| | ♥ K J 9 7 4 | |
| | ♦ A 8 3 | |
| | ♣ 10 8 | |
| West | | East |
| ♠ 8 2 | | ♠ J 10 9 6 |
| ♥ Q 6 5 | | ♥ 10 8 |
| ♦ Q 9 7 4 | | ♦ J 10 6 5 |
| ♣ Q 9 6 5 | | ♣ A K 2 |
| | South | |
| | ♠ A 7 4 3 | |
| | ♥ A 3 2 | |
| | ♦ K 2 | |
| | ♣ J 7 4 3 | |

| Bidding: | West | North | East | South |
|---|---|---|---|---|
| | ---- | 1♥ | Pass | 1♠ |
| | Pass | 2♠ | Pass | 4♥ |
| | All Pass | | | |
| Opening Lead: ♣A | | | | |

In this hand, both tactics succeed and you make an overtrick.

64

# DECLARER PLANNING
## SUIT CONTRACT CHECK LIST

- [ ] WHAT'S MY CONTRACT?
- [ ] HOW MANY TRICKS DO I NEED?
- [ ] HOW MANY LOSERS DO I HAVE?
  - [ ] SURE LOSERS?
  - [ ] POSSIBLE LOSERS?

*IF TOO MANY FOR MY CONTRACT TO SUCCEED,*

- [ ] HOW CAN I AVOID SOME LOSERS?
  - [ ] RUFFING
  - [ ] FINESSING
  - [ ] DISCARDING ON WINNERS IN ANOTHER SUIT
  - [ ] SETTING UP LONG SUIT
  - [ ] OTHERS

- [ ] WHAT HAVE I LEARNED FROM OPPONENTS' BIDDING?
- [ ] DO I DRAW TRUMPS IMMEDIATELY?
- [ ] DO I DELAY DRAWING TRUMPS?
- [ ] DOES IT ALL ADD UP TO ENOUGH TRICKS FOR MY CONTRACT?

N.L.

## RUFFING LOSERS

The primary advantage of a suit contract over notrump is its ability to generate tricks by trumping defenders' high cards, which otherwise would be losers. The suit contract has the extra safety valve of being able to "stop" the opponents from running a long suit. This intrinsic benefit should be in the forefront of your mind when you, as declarer, plan the play of the hand.

---

Dealer: East

| West | East |
|------|------|
| ♠ K 9 8 7 5 | ♠ A 6 4 2 |
| ♥ 6 3 | ♥ Q 8 5 4 |
| ♦ A 10 5 | ♦ 6 |
| ♣ A K 5 | ♣ Q 6 3 2 |

| Bidding: | West | North | East | South |
|----------|------|-------|------|-------|
| | --- | --- | Pass | Pass |
| | 1♠ | 2♦ | 3♠ | Pass |
| | 4♠ | All Pass | | |

Opening Lead: ♦K

---

The opening lead of the ♦K has been made, dummy's hand has been tabled and your planning of the play commences.

## THE PLANNING

■ I need 10 tricks for my 4♠ contract.

■ Sure losers:  Hearts: Two
                Clubs: None

■ Possible losers:  Diamonds: Two
                    Spades: Two

66

■ How can I avoid some of my losers?

■ I can ruff two of my diamonds in dummy. Dummy has a singleton diamond.

■ The opponents' trumps may divide 2-2, in which case I'll have no losers there. If they break 3-1, I'll have only one loser. If the break is 4-0, I'm in big trouble.

■ I could possibly set up a long club as a trick, if I could get a 3-3 break, for a discard. But that's a long shot.

■ Do I draw trumps immediately? I can safely draw two rounds of trump, because I need only two of dummy's trumps to ruff my diamond losers.

■ Does it add up to enough tricks for my contract?

| | |
|---|---|
| Spades (trumps): | 4 tricks (if suit breaks 3-1) |
| Hearts: | None |
| Diamonds: | 3 (the ace plus two ruffs in dummy) |
| Clubs: | 3 tricks (minimum) |
| Total | 10 tricks |

## THE PLAY

How do you proceed?

1. Win opening lead with ♦A.
2. Draw two rounds of trump, ace and king. If the opponents' trumps divide 2-2, great. If not, stop drawing trumps, allowing the opponents' high trump to remain outstanding.
3. Ruff a diamond in dummy.
4. Return to hand with ♣K.
5. Ruff another diamond.
6. Play ♣A. Then lead to dummy's ♣Q. If suit breaks 3-3, play dummy's last club discarding a heart. If that works you make at least five. If not, you make four.

You've given your hand every possibility of success.

The complete hand:

| | North | |
|---|---|---|
| | ♠ 10 | |
| | ♥ A 7 2 | |
| | ♦ K Q J 4 3 | |
| | ♣ J 10 9 4 | |
| West | | East |
| ♠ K 9 8 7 5 | | ♠ A 6 4 2 |
| ♥ 6 3 | | ♥ Q 8 5 4 |
| ♦ A 10 5 | | ♦ 6 |
| ♣ A K 5 | | ♣ Q 6 3 2 |
| | South | |
| | ♠ Q J 3 | |
| | ♥ K J 10 9 | |
| | ♦ 9 8 7 2 | |
| | ♣ 8 7 | |

Declarer: West
Contract: 4♠

In the actual case, as shown above, the correct play will bring in your contract on the nose: 10 tricks. You lose one spade and two heart tricks.

You will note that if you had drawn three rounds of trump before ruffing *both* your diamond losers, you would have been defeated.

### DISCARDING LOSERS ON HIGH CARDS IN OTHER SUITS

Getting rid of losers often can be accomplished by discarding them on high cards in a different suit or suits. The setup that is required for this maneuver is to have shortness of a suit in one hand and high cards in the same suit, with greater length, in the other hand.

The following examples illustrate how this principle can work.
The contract is: 4♠
The opening lead is: ♣K
In each of the four examples your 4♠ contract, requiring 10 tricks, can permit three losers.

| 1. | Partner |
|---|---|
| | ♠ K 6 4 2 |
| | ♥ A 6 5 |
| | ♦ 4 |
| | ♣ 9 6 5 4 2 |
| | |
| | You |
| | ♠ A Q J 5 3 |
| | ♥ 9 8 4 |
| | ♦ A K 7 |
| | ♣ 7 3 |

*THE PLANNING:*

| | |
|---|---|
| Clubs: | Two sure losers. |
| Diamonds: | One possible loser. |
| Hearts: | Two possible losers. |
| Spades: | No losers. |

What can you do about the five potential losers?

Diamonds: You can ruff one diamond in dummy.

Hearts: You can discard one of dummy's hearts on one of your high diamonds. This allows you to ruff a heart in dummy after relinquishing a trick in the suit.

Can you draw trumps first?

You need two trumps in dummy for ruffing purposes. You also need trumps for communications. The most you can draw is one round of trump. You have to take care of your other chores first.

## THE PLAY:

You lose the first two club tricks and win the heart switch with dummy's ace. You can draw one round of trump with your queen and hope each defender follows. Play the ♦A followed by the ♦K on which you discard one of dummy's hearts. Ruff your last diamond in dummy, and give up a heart trick. Win any return, ruff your last heart in dummy and now draw all the trumps.

♦ ♦ ♦ ♦

| 2. | Partner |
|---|---|
| | ♠9 6 3 2 |
| | ♥K 7 |
| | ♦A 5 4 |
| | ♣10 9 7 6 |
| | |
| | You |
| | ♠A K 7 5 4 |
| | ♥A Q 3 |
| | ♦K 8 6 |
| | ♣8 3 |

## THE PLANNING:

Clubs: Two sure losers.
Diamonds: One possible loser.
Hearts: No losers.
Spades: One possible loser.

What can you do about the potential losers?
You can discard a diamond in dummy on a high heart.
Do you draw trumps?
You can safely draw two rounds of trump. You need only one trump in dummy to ruff a diamond loser.

70

## THE PLAY:

The opening club lead is continued as the defense wins two tricks and you ruff the third.

Play two rounds of trump. If the suit splits 2-2, you lose no tricks. If it's 3-1, you leave the outstanding trump with the opponents.

You now play three rounds of hearts, winning the king first, followed by the ace and queen. On the queen you discard a small diamond from dummy.

A small diamond is played to dummy's ace, back to your king and you ruff the third diamond in dummy.

You've made 11 tricks if trumps broke 2-2, 10 tricks if they broke 3-1. (Bring out the crying towel, if they broke 4-0.)

♦ ♦ ♦ ♦

| 3. | Partner |
|---|---|
| | ♠ A 9 6 3 2 |
| | ♥ 7 6 4 |
| | ♦ — |
| | ♣ 9 8 7 5 3 |
| | |
| | You |
| | ♠ K 8 7 5 4 |
| | ♥ A 8 2 |
| | ♦ A K 2 |
| | ♣ 6 2 |

## THE PLANNING

Clubs: Two sure losers.
Diamonds: One possible loser.
Hearts: Two possible losers.
Spades: One possible loser (with 3-0 break).

71

What can you do about potential losers?

Diamonds: You can ruff one loser in dummy. Hearts: you can discard two of dummy's hearts on your ace-king of diamonds. You will then be able to ruff your two small hearts in dummy.

Do you draw trumps? You can afford to draw two rounds of trump. You need only three trumps in dummy to ruff your two heart losers and a diamond.

## THE PLAY

After the opponents cash their first two clubs, you ruff the third lead of the suit.

Draw two rounds of trump, making sure to win the second trump in your hand. If they break 2-1, you have no trump losers. If they break 3-0 you will have an eventual loser.

Now cash your ♦A K discarding dummy's two small hearts. Ruff a diamond in dummy. Play to your ♥A and then ruff a small heart in dummy. Ruff a club in your hand and your last heart in dummy. You've made 11 tricks if trump had broken favorably or 10 tricks with a poor trump break

♦ ♦ ♦ ♦

4.

| | Partner |
| --- | --- |
| | ♠ A J 9 8 |
| | ♥ A 7 2 |
| | ♦ K Q J 10 |
| | ♣ 8 2 |

| | You |
| --- | --- |
| | ♠ K Q 6 3 2 |
| | ♥ 9 6 3 |
| | ♦ 6 |
| | ♣ A 7 6 3 |

## THE PLANNING

Clubs: One sure plus two possible losers. Diamonds: One loser. Hearts: Two possible losers. Spades: No losers.

With a club opening lead you have a guaranteed loser there. You also cannot do anything about your diamond loser. The only hope is to set up dummy's diamond honors for discards of your heart losers, and if necessary, for a club loser.

Do you lead trump? Yes and no. You can afford to play the trump ace. If both defenders follow suit you can continue to draw all the opponents' trumps. If the suit breaks 4-0, you should stop at this point. You have to retain dummy's spades to ruff any club continuation.

## THE PLAY

Win the opening lead with your ace. Test the trump situation by cashing the ♠A. If both defenders follow, as is most likely, then draw the balance of the trumps.

Give up a diamond trick to the ace. When clubs are continued you lose one trick, then ruff the next round of the suit. Dummy's three set-up diamond honors are cashed, discarding two hearts and a club.

You've made 11 tricks, losing only a club and a diamond.

How would you handle this hand?

---

Dealer: South

North
♠ Q J 9 2
♥ K Q 7 5 2
♦ 10 9 6
♣ 5

South
♠ K 10 8 5 3
♥ 6 3
♦ A 4 3
♣ A K 9

| Bidding: | West | North | East | South |
|---|---|---|---|---|
| | — | — | — | 1♠ |
| | Pass | 2♥ | Pass | 2NT |
| | Pass | 3♠ | Pass | 4♠ |
| | All Pass | | | |

Opening Lead: ♦K

---

## THE PLANNING

How many sure losers do you have?

How many possible losers do you have?

Do they add up to more losers than you can afford for your contract?

If so, how can you eliminate some of your possible losers?

Are there any finesse possibilities?

Can you discard any losers on high cards?

Can you ruff any losers?

Should you draw trumps immediately?

74

Sure losers: Spades: One loser.
                       Hearts: One loser.
      Possible losers: Diamonds: Two losers.
                               Clubs: One loser.
                               Total: Five losers.

Survey the ways to avoid some possible losers.
Finesses: None
Discard losers on high cards: Discard a diamond from dummy
on a high club.
Ruffing: You can ruff a club in dummy and eventually a dia-
mond.
Draw trumps immediately?
No. If you draw trumps first, the opponents will grab their
trump ace and then cash two top diamonds and a heart.

## THE PLAY

```
                         North
                         ♠ Q J 9 2
                         ♥ K Q 7 5 2
                         ♦ 10 9 6
                         ♣ 5
         West                          East
         ♠ A 6 4                       ♠ 7
         ♥ 9 8                         ♥ A J 10 4
         ♦ K Q J 2                     ♦ 8 7 5
         ♣ Q 8 7 4                     ♣ J 10 6 3 2
                         South
                         ♠ K 10 8 5 3
                         ♥ 6 3
                         ♦ A 4 3
                         ♣ A K 9

      Contract: 4♠ by South
      Opening Lead: ♦K
```

75

Win the opening lead with your ♦A. Play the ♣ A K, discarding a diamond from dummy. Ruff the ♣9 in dummy. Give up a diamond trick to the defenders. If defenders play hearts, they will win the ace and return the suit, you win it in dummy. Play a small spade to your 8. If it wins, ruff your last diamond in dummy and now draw the balance of the trumps. (If West had won the first spade trick and returned another spade, you would have won it in your hand and ruffed your diamond in dummy.) You make your contract, losing one spade, one heart and one diamond trick.

If you had prematurely led even one trump before relinquishing your lead in diamonds, you would have been defeated. All West had to do was hold off winning the first trump trick. Then upon gaining the lead in the diamond suit, West would play the ace and a small trump removing all of dummy's trumps. You no longer could ruff your diamond loser in dummy.

♦ ♦ ♦ ♦

## ELIMINATING LOSERS BY FINESSING

We've discussed various techniques of the finesse. Let's see how it works in this suit contract.

| West | | | East |
|------|------|------|------|
| ♠ J 10 9 6 | | | ♠ A Q 8 5 4 |
| ♥ 10 7 6 | | | ♥ K Q J |
| ♦ K J 10 | | | ♦ 8 7 2 |
| ♣ A 4 2 | | | ♣ K 5 |

| Bidding: | West | North | East | South |
|----------|------|-------|------|-------|
| | Pass | Pass | 1♠ | Pass |
| | 2♠ | Pass | 3♠ | Pass |
| | 4♠ | All Pass | | |

Contract: 4♠
Opening Lead: ♣J

## THE PLANNING

    Spades: One possible loser.
    Hearts: One sure loser.
  Diamonds: One sure loser and one possible loser.
    Clubs: No losers.

How can I eliminate one or more losers?
Can I afford to draw trumps first?
Are any finesses possible? In which suits?
Where should I win the first trick?

## THE PLAY

Win the opening lead in dummy with the ace.

Start drawing trumps immediately. Lead the ♠J. If North doesn't cover, let it ride. (If the finesse wins, try it again by leading the 10.)

If it loses, win the expected club return in your hand. Play high trumps from your hand if necessary to draw the balance of the trumps.

Now attempt the diamond finesse.
Lead a small diamond from your hand. If South plays small, finesse with the 10.

A.  If it loses to North's queen you're sunk.
B.  If, however, it loses to North's ace, ruff the expected club return and try the finesse again. If it succeeds, as it now should, you have eliminated one of your diamond losers.
C.  If your initial finesse of the 10 succeeded, return to your hand by ruffing a club. Now repeat the finesse again, covering any card South plays. If it's a small card, play the jack; if it's the queen play the king; if it's the ace, naturally, you play small.

77

The complete hand:

```
                    North
                    ♠ 3
                    ♥ 8 5 3 2
                    ♦ A 9 4 3
                    ♣ Q 8 6 3
    West                              East
    ♠ J 10 9 6                        ♠ A Q 8 5 4
    ♥ 10 7 6                          ♥ K Q J
    ♦ K J 10                          ♦ 8 7 2
    ♣ A 4 2                           ♣ K 5
                    South
                    ♠ K 7 2
                    ♥ A 9 4
                    ♦ Q 6 5
                    ♣ J 10 9 7
```

You had two chances to make the contract. If the spade finesse succeeded, you made the contract. If the diamond finesse worked, you made the contract. If both succeeded you wound up with an overtrick. If *both* failed, you lost, but the odds were very much in your favor.

♦ ♦ ♦ ♦

## SETTING UP A LONG SUIT FOR DISCARDING LOSERS

In our opening statement we discussed how high cards, ruffing and long suits win tricks. Let's see how the latter can work for you in suit contracts when you use the proper techniques.

```
Dealer: North
                        North
                        ♠ J 9
                        ♥ K 9 3
                        ♦ A 9 8 6 3
                        ♣ 6 5 3

                        South
                        ♠ 5 4
                        ♥ A Q 6 5 2
                        ♦ K 5 4
                        ♣ A K 7
```

| Bidding: | West | North | East | South |
|----------|------|-------|------|-------|
|          | ---  | Pass  | Pass | 1♥    |
|          | Pass | 2♥    | Pass | 3♥    |
|          | Pass | 4♥    | All Pass |    |

Opening Lead: ♠K

## PLANNING

With the 4♥ contract, you can afford to lose only three tricks.
How many sure losers? How many potential losers are there?
How can you eliminate some losers?
Ruffing? Finesses? Discards on high cards?
Setting up a long suit for discards?
Can you draw trumps immediately?

With the opening lead you have two sure spade losers staring
you in the face, plus a potential diamond and a club loser. If you
get a reasonable 3-2 trump break, you have no losers there.

There are no ruffing or finesse possibilities and no high cards
available for discards. All that is left is the five-card diamond
suit to be set up for a discard of your club loser.

```
Dealer: North
                        North
                        ♠ J 9
                        ♥ K 9 3
                        ♦ A 9 8 6 3
                        ♣ 6 5 3
        West                            East
        ♠ K Q 10 8                      ♠ A 7 6 3 2
        ♥ 10 8 4                        ♥ J 7
        ♦ 10 7                          ♦ Q J 2
        ♣ Q J 10 8                      ♣ 9 4 2
                        South
                        ♠ 5 4
                        ♥ A Q 6 5 2
                        ♦ K 5 4
                        ♣ A K 7
Contract: 4♥ by South
Opening Lead: ♠K
```

## THE PLAY

The opponents cash two spade tricks and switch to the ♣Q, which you win with your king. Your hopes are to get normal 3-2 breaks in both the trump and diamond suits.

Under these circumstances it is wise to draw the opponents' trumps in three rounds. When that succeeds you turn your attention to the diamond suit. Care must be taken here. You have only one entry to dummy, the ♦A

Play the ♦K and then a small card to dummy's 8, expecting to surrender the trick to the defense.

If the suit divided 3-2, you win the expected club return. Play your diamond to dummy's ace. The suit is now set up. Cash a diamond winner and discard your club loser.

You've made your contract, losing just two spades and one diamond.

(A little sidelight: Your method of playing the diamond suit had an extra chance of success even if the diamonds broke 4-1, with West holding the four cards and East having a singleton honor.)

The East-West hands might be something like this:

| West | East |
|------|------|
| ♠ K Q 10 8 | ♠ A 7 6 3 2 |
| ♥ 10 8 | ♥ J 7 4 |
| ♦ Q J 7 2 | ♦ 10 |
| ♣ Q J 10 | ♣ 9 8 4 2 |

After winning the ♦K, felling East's honor, you duck when West splits his honors on your next lead. Upon regaining the lead, you have a proven finesse against his remaining diamond honor. This promotes a diamond trick which enables you to discard a club loser in your hand. Try it.

♦ ♦ ♦ ♦

# CHAPTER 5

# DECLARER PLAY
# IN SUIT CONTRACTS
### (Continued)

## WHEN TO DRAW TRUMPS
## &
## WHEN TO DELAY DRAWING TRUMPS

*Guidelines to help choose the correct route.*

♦ ♦ ♦

*DRAWING TRUMPS*
*to protect high cards*
*and side suits*
*from being ruffed*
*by defenders.*

♦ ♦ ♦

*DELAYING DRAWING TRUMPS*
*to be able to ruff*
*defenders' high cards,*
*to provide entries*
*and*
*to maintain control*
*of the hand.*

TO DRAW
OR
NOT TO DRAW... ooo

Do I draw trumps first or do I delay playing trumps until later? These questions continually perplex many declarers.

The answers will often come as you do your planning before playing to the first trick. So what are some guidelines for making the correct choice: *To draw or not to draw?*

## WHEN TO DRAW TRUMPS
Drawing trumps is usually a very good idea. The key is to recognize the conditions when it is safe to do so.

1. You have high cards or a long side suit which you want to protect against ruffs.

2. You have ample trumps to maintain control of the hand.

3. You have sufficient trumps in the short hand (usually dummy) to take care of ruffing after drawing trumps.

Let's look at these hands:

1.

| | | Partner | | |
|---|---|---|---|---|
| | | ♠ 6 5 4 | | |
| | | ♥ A J 2 | | |
| | | ♦ K Q 7 6 3 | | |
| | | ♣ 7 6 | | |
| | | | | |
| | | You | | |
| | | ♠ 7 2 | | |
| | | ♥ K Q 9 6 5 | | |
| | | ♦ A J 4 | | |
| | | ♣ A 4 2 | | |

| Bidding: | West | North | East | South |
|---|---|---|---|---|
| | ---- | ---- | ---- | 1♥ |
| | 1♠ | 2♦ | Pass | 3♦ |
| | Pass | 3♥ | Pass | 4♥ |
| | All Pass | | | |

Opening Lead: ♠K

### THE PLANNING

Sure losers: two tricks in spades.
Possible losers: two tricks in clubs.
What can I do about my possible losers?
Ruffing? Finesses? Discard on high cards in another suit?
Discard on a long suit?
What have I learned from the bidding?
Do I draw trumps?

As you look at your options for getting rid of losers, you might give a fleeting glance at the possibility of ruffing a club in dummy. But that involves giving up a trick in the suit and risking overruffs as well.

85

A more practical solution is discarding club losers on that long, strong diamond suit in dummy. But you can't run a long side suit and allow defenders to retain trumps at the same time. So the answer is, "Yes, I draw the trumps first."

### THE PLAY

The defense cashes ♠A K and switches to the ♣K, which you win. Lead a small trump to dummy's ace. When both defenders follow suit, you know that trumps will break no worse than 4-1. You can safely draw the balance of the trumps, and then go about the business of setting up the diamond suit. If the suit divides at the worst, 4-1, you will make 11 tricks. If it breaks a miserable 5-0, you will still make 10 tricks for the contract.

♦ ♦ ♦ ♦ ♦

2.

♠ A J 9 6
♥ 7 6 4 2
♦ 8 5
♣ A Q J

You

♠ K Q 10 5 3
♥ 8 3
♦ A K 7
♣ 8 6 5

| Bidding: | West | North | East | South |
|---|---|---|---|---|
| | ---- | ---- | Pass | 1♠ |
| | Pass | 3♠ | Pass | 4♠ |
| | All Pass | | | |

Opening Lead: ♥K

## THE PLANNING

Sure losers: two hearts.
Possible losers: one diamond, one club.

Getting rid of losers: Finesses? Ruffing?
Discarding on high cards?

Finesse: Yes, in the club suit.
Ruffing: Yes, ruff a diamond in dummy.
There are no high cards available for discarding.

Should I draw trumps first?

Yes, I should attempt to draw trumps immediately. If they break no worse than 3-1, it is safe to draw trumps. Only one trump in dummy is necessary to ruff a diamond loser.

## THE PLAY

The defenders cash two heart tricks and you ruff the third.

Test the trump suit by playing to dummy's ace. If both defenders follow, continue to draw the opponents' trumps, winding up in your own hand.

Take the club finesse. If it wins, return to your hand with the ♦K and repeat the club finesse. If it is successful again, play a diamond to your ace and then ruff a diamond in dummy. You wind up making 11 tricks. (If the club finesse had lost, you'd have made 10 tricks.)

♦ ♦ ♦ ♦ ♦

Plan and play this hand:

```
Dealer: North
                        North
                        ♠ A K 10 6 2
                        ♥ Q 10
                        ♦ Q J 9
                        ♣ K 3 2

                        South
                        ♠ Q J 9 3
                        ♥ 7 5 4 2
                        ♦ K 10
                        ♣ A 7 4
```

| Bidding: | West | North | East | South |
|----------|------|-------|------|-------|
|          | ---- | 1♠    | 2♥   | 2♠    |
|          | Pass | 3♠    | Pass | 4♠    |
|          | All Pass |   |      |       |

Opening Lead: ♥A

## THE PLANNING

Sure losers:     Two tricks in hearts.
                    One trick in diamonds.
Possible losers:  One trick in clubs

How do I get rid of some losers?
Do I draw trumps immediately?

## THE PLAY

Defenders win ♥A K and then switch to a club.
How do you continue?

88

The complete hand:

```
                          North
                          ♠ A K 10 6 2
                          ♥ Q 10
                          ♦ Q J 9
                          ♣ K 3 2
        West                                East
        ♠ 5                                 ♠ 8 7 4
        ♥ 3                                 ♥ A K J 9 8 6
        ♦ A 5 4 3 2                         ♦ 8 7 6
        ♣ Q J 10 9 8 5                      ♣ 6
                          South
                          ♠ Q J 9 3
                          ♥ 7 5 4 2
                          ♦ K 10
                          ♣ A 7 4

Contract: 4♠ by North
Opening Lead:  ♥A
```

After the opponents cash their two heart winners and switch to a club, you win the trick with dummy's ace.

Although your strategy is to discard a club loser on a set-up high diamond honor, you can afford to draw trumps first.

You cash dummy's ♠Q. When both defenders follow you can safely play up to three rounds, depleting opponents' trumps. Now you go about setting up diamonds. Lead the ♦K. West wins and returns the ♣Q which your ♣K wins. Play your high ♦Q and ♦J on which you discard dummy's club loser. Ruff your last club with dummy's last trump. You've fulfilled your contract, losing two hearts and one diamond.

Notice what would have happened if you did not draw trumps immediately. You would have played the ♦K to set up your lower honors. West would have won with the ace and played a club for East to ruff, setting the contract.

1. YOU NEED DUMMY'S TRUMPS TO RUFF YOUR LOSERS IN A SIDE SUIT.

2. YOU AND DUMMY ARE SHORT IN TWO DIFFERENT SIDE SUITS... A CROSS-RUFF HAND.

3. YOU HAVE QUICK LOSERS TO DISCARD ON HIGH CARDS AND YOU'D HAVE TO GIVE UP THE LEAD IF YOU DREW TRUMPS.

4. YOU NEED DUMMY'S TRUMPS AS ENTRIES:
   - TO SET UP A SIDE SUIT
   - TO ALTERNATE PULLING TRUMPS AND TAKING FINESSES.

5. TO MAINTAIN CONTROL OF THE HAND.

## WHEN TO DELAY DRAWING TRUMPS

The concepts behind knowing when to delay drawing trumps are a bit more sophisticated. The accompanying chart indicates some of the main guidelines you should look for.

♦ ♦ ♦ ♦ ♦

## YOU NEED DUMMY'S TRUMPS TO RUFF LOSERS

Dummy is short in a side suit. You have losers in your hand in the same suit. If you drew the trumps first, you would not have sufficient trumps in dummy to take care of your losers.

```
Example 1.
                        Dummy
                        ♠ 6
                        ♥ A 6 5
                        ♦ K 8 2
                        ♣ 10 9 8 7 4 3

                        You
                        ♠ A 8 5
                        ♥ K Q 10 8 3
                        ♦ A Q 4
                        ♣ 6 5
Contract: 4♥
Opening Lead: ♠K
```

The spade opening lead exposes the hand to two spade and two club losers. Dummy's two small trumps are needed to ruff your spade losers. The play would simply go, win the ♠A, ruff a spade in dummy. Return to your hand with a diamond, ruff another spade in dummy. Cash the trump ace. Return to your hand again with a diamond to your ace. Draw the balance of the trumps. If the opponents' trumps broke 3-1 you made 11 tricks, losing only two clubs.

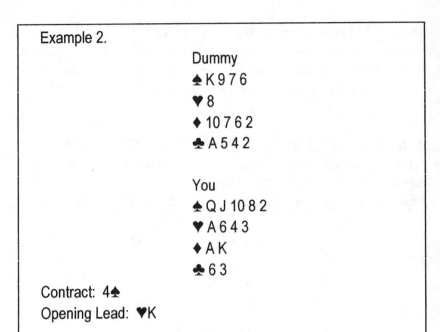

Example 2.

                    Dummy
                    ♠ K 9 7 6
                    ♥ 8
                    ♦ 10 7 6 2
                    ♣ A 5 4 2

                    You
                    ♠ Q J 10 8 2
                    ♥ A 6 4 3
                    ♦ A K
                    ♣ 6 3

Contract: 4♠
Opening Lead: ♥K

The ♥K is won by your ace. You now have three heart losers, one club loser as well as one trump.

Your shortness of hearts in dummy will permit ruffing your losers there. Upon winning the opening lead, play a small heart and ruff it in dummy. Return to your hand with a diamond and ruff another heart in dummy. If it is not over ruffed, cash your ♣A in dummy. Enter your hand once more with a diamond and repeat attempting to ruff your last heart in dummy. If all has gone well, you will lose only two tricks, the ace of trump and a club.

Even if your first or second attempt at trumping hearts in dummy is overruffed, the opponents are capturing the trick with the trump ace, a winner for them in any event.

If the defenders are astute enough to return a trump at this point, the worst that has happened is that you were held to your contract, losing one trick each in the spade, heart and club suits.

Note what could have happened if you had initially attempted to draw trumps before embarking on your tactic of ruffing hearts in dummy.

A sophisticated defender, holding three spades to the ace, could permit you to win the first trump lead. Upon your second lead he would grab the ace and play another spade reducing your dummy trump holding to only one card. Your losses would have been *two* hearts, one spade and one club.

♦ ♦ ♦ ♦ ♦

## CROSS-RUFF THE HAND

When you and the dummy are short in two different side suits, many additional tricks can be attained by playing the hand as a cross-ruff.

This is an important instance where it is usually wise *not* to draw trumps. The trumps in each hand can be better utilized individually.

| Example: | | |
| --- | --- | --- |
| | Dummy | You |
| (Trump Suit) | A J 8 7 | K Q 10 9 6 |

If you simply play your trumps, the most you can win is five tricks. However, if used as a cross-ruff, you can conceivably win four tricks in dummy and five in your hand, a total of nine tricks.

What is the best way to handle this setup?

| Dummy | You |
| --- | --- |
| ♠ K J 4 2 | ♠ 6 3 |
| ♥ Q 10 8 3 | ♥ A K J 7 4 |
| ♦ 7 | ♦ A 6 5 4 2 |
| ♣ A 7 5 3 | ♣ 8 |

You're in a 4♥ contract. The opening lead is ♣K.

## THE PLANNING:

You have two possible spade losers and four possible diamond losers.

There is a possibility of a finesse in spades. Dummy is short in diamonds. You have an opportunity to ruff your long diamonds in dummy.

You also have club shortness in your hand. That can be a convenient way of reaching your hand to play diamonds to ruff in dummy. This looks like a good time to employ the cross-ruff tactic.

Let's see how you play the hand.

```
Dealer: East
                        North
                        ♠ A Q
                        ♥ 9 6 2
                        ♦ K Q J 9
                        ♣ J 6 4 2

        West                            East
        ♠ K J 4 2                       ♠ 6 3
        ♥ Q 10 8 3                      ♥ A K J 7 4
        ♦ 7                             ♦ A 6 5 4 2
        ♣ A 7 5 3                       ♣ 8

                        South
                        ♠ 10 9 8 7 5
                        ♥ 5
                        ♦ 10 8 3
                        ♣ K Q 10 9
```

| Bidding: | West | North | East | South: |
|----------|------|-------|------|--------|
|          | ---- | ----  | 1♥   | Pass   |
|          | 3♥   | Pass  | 4♥   | All Pass |

Opening Lead: ♣K

## *THE PLAY*:

You win the opening lead with dummy's ♣A. Your goal is to try to ruff four diamonds in dummy. To utilize entries into your hand to the fullest, you start on the diamond suit immediately. Play a diamond to your ace and ruff a diamond in dummy. Now ruff a club in your hand and alternate ruffing diamonds in dummy and clubs in your hand. You wind up in dummy with this situation:

```
                    North
                    ♠ A
                    ♥ 9 6 2
     West                          East
     ♠ K J 4 2                     ♠ 6 3
     ♥ ----                        ♥ A K
                    South
                    ♠ 10 9 8
                    ♥ 5
```

You have already won nine tricks, five diamonds and four clubs. You must win your A K of trumps, eleven tricks in all.

♦ ♦ ♦ ♦ ♦

## DISCARD QUICK LOSERS

There are times when you have sufficient trumps to pull them safely, but you have other problems that have priorities.

Here is a simple example:

---

North
♠ 9 7 2
♥ Q J 9 3
♦ Q 7
♣ K Q 4 3

South
♠ A 8 6
♥ K 10 8 7 6
♦ A K 8
♣ 8 2

Contract: 4♥
Opening Lead: ♣J

---

On the opening ♣J you play dummy's queen and East wins with the ace. He switches to the ♠K.

At this point you've lost one club trick, you have a sure loser in trumps, and two exposed losers in spades.

If you try to draw trumps at this juncture, the opponents will grab the ace and cash two spade tricks, defeating the contract.

How do you proceed?

Complete Hand:

```
Dealer: South
                          North
                          ♠ 9 7 2
                          ♥ Q J 9 3
                          ♦ Q 7
                          ♣ K Q 4 3

        West                              East
        ♠ 10 4 3                          ♠ K Q J 5
        ♥ A 5                             ♥ 4 2
        ♦ J 9 5 3                         ♦ 10 6 4 2
        ♣ J 10 9 7                        ♣ A 6 5

                          South
                          ♠ A 8 6
                          ♥ K 10 8 7 6
                          ♦ A K 8
                          ♣ 8 2
```

| Bidding: | West | North | East | South |
|----------|------|-------|------|-------|
|          | ---- | ----  | ---- | 1♥    |
|          | Pass | 2♣    | Pass | 2 NT  |
|          | Pass | 3♥    | Pass | 4♥    |
|          | All Pass |    |      |       |

Opening Lead: ♣J

## DISCARDING A LOSER BEFORE DRAWING TRUMPS

You must delay playing trumps and look for a way to get rid of one of your spade losers. Fortunately, the diamond suit can provide the means. With only two diamonds in dummy and a combination of A K Q in the combined hands, you can discard a spade loser on the third diamond. Play a small diamond to dummy's queen, then back to your king, followed by the ace on which you discard a spade from dummy.

97

You now give up a spade to the opponents. If a club is returned to dummy's queen, you play a small trump to your hand. Assuming that the opponents win the ace, you win any return (a trump or a club) in your hand. Ruff your last spade in dummy and play a high trump from dummy. All you have left in your hand are high trumps. You've fulfilled your contract, losing one club, one spade and one trump.

♦ ♦ ♦ ♦ ♦

## YOU NEED DUMMY'S TRUMPS AS ENTRIES TO ESTABLISH AND REACH WINNERS

Another valid reason to delay drawing trumps is to retain dummy's trumps as entries. At times, you can set up high cards or a long suit in dummy, but you have no outside entries to cash them, other than in the trump suit.

Consider this hand:

| North |
|---|
| ♠ 9 7 |
| ♥ A J 10 |
| ♦ A 9 8 7 5 |
| ♣ 7 5 4 |

| South |
|---|
| ♠ Q J |
| ♥ K Q 9 7 4 2 |
| ♦ K 3 |
| ♣ A 8 6 |

Contract: 4♥ by South
Opening Lead: ♣K

## PLANNING:

Your contract permits only three losers.
With the opening lead forcing your ♣A, you have two spades and two club losers exposed to capture.

How can you eliminate one of the losers?
Are there any finesses possible?
Are there any high cards available to obtain discards?
The answer is "NO" in both cases.

Is there a long suit you can set up for discards?
Yes, the diamond suit has possibilities.

How many discards do you need?
Just one for the contract to succeed.

What division of the opponents' diamonds do you require?
No worse than 4-2.

Can you draw trumps immediately?
No. You may need them for entries to dummy when the suit is set up.

## THE PLAY:

Win the opening lead with the ♣A. Immediately go after the diamond suit. Play your king. Then a small diamond to dummy's ace. Ruff a small diamond with your *queen of trumps*. If both players follow suit, the diamonds are set up. But, as is more likely, the suit breaks 4-2. You have to reach dummy with a trump and ruff another diamond with your trump king.

Now play another trump to dummy. If the trump suit doesn't break 2-2, you play one more high trump from dummy, drawing the defenders' final trump. You are safely in dummy's hand and play your good diamond, discarding a club loser from your hand.

You make 4♥, losing two spades and one club.

The Complete Hand:

```
Dealer: South
                          North
                          ♠ 9 7
                          ♥ A J 10
                          ♦ A 9 8 7 5
                          ♣ 7 5 4
        West                                East
        ♠ K 8 6 4 2                         ♠ A 10 5 3
        ♥ 8 3                               ♥ 6 5
        ♦ 6 2                               ♦ Q J 10 4
        ♣ K Q J 9                           ♣ 10 3 2

                          South
                          ♠ Q J
                          ♥ K Q 9 7 4 2
                          ♦ K 3
                          ♣ A 8 6
```

| Bidding: | West | North | East | South |
|----------|------|-------|------|-------|
|          | ---- | ----  | ---- | 1♥    |
|          | Pass | 2♥    | Pass | 3♥    |
|          | Pass | 4♥    | All Pass |   |

Opening Lead: ♣K

In the actual hand, the key diamond suit broke 4-2, necessitating extra entries into dummy. Note that if you drew the trumps immediately and then worked on the diamonds, you could have set up the suit, but you would not have an entry to dummy to cash the winning diamonds.

## DELAY DRAWING TRUMPS TO REACH HIGH CARDS

Whereas the problem in the previous hand was to establish and reach a long suit, similar considerations are involved in the setting up of high cards.

```
                    Dummy
                    ♠ K 6 5
                    ♥ K Q J 2
                    ♦ 8 6 3
                    ♣ 9 4 3

                    You
                    ♠ A Q J 7 4
                    ♥ 7 4
                    ♦ A 7 5
                    ♣ A K 6
Contract: 4♠
Opening Lead: ♦K
```

## PLANNING:

The opening lead has exposed your two small diamonds as losers. You have a sure heart loser and a possible club loser.

1. How can you avoid one loser?
2  Should you draw all the opponents' trumps immediately? If not, why not?

1. The heart suit can provide the answer. You have only two hearts in your hand, but you have *three* big honors in dummy. By surrendering the king to the defenders' ace you can establish the queen and jack as winners. On the jack you can discard your losing club.
2. Against reasonably good defenders you should *not* draw all their trumps immediately. You may need an entry to dummy to cash the ♥J for a discard.

101

The Complete Hand:

Dealer: South

North
♠ K 6 5
♥ K Q J 2
♦ 8 6 3
♣ 9 4 3

West
♠ 9 8
♥ A 6 5
♦ K Q J 9 2
♣ 8 5 2

East
♠ 10 3 2
♥ 10 9 8 3
♦ 10 4
♣ Q J 10 7

South
♠ A Q J 7 4
♥ 7 4
♦ A 7 5
♣ A K 6

| Bidding: | West | North | East | South |
|----------|------|-------|------|-------|
|          | ---- | ----  | ---- | 1♠    |
|          | Pass | 2♠    | Pass | 4♠    |
|          | All Pass |   |      |       |

Opening Lead: ♦K

## THE PLAY:

Win the ♦K with your ace. Draw *one round* of trump with your queen, Now play a small heart. If West takes the trick your problems are probably over. But a good defender will refuse to win this first heart lead.

When that occurs, you play *one* more trump to your hand, leaving the trump king in dummy.

Lead a second heart which West must now win. The defense can cash their two diamond winners. You win any return in

102

your hand and play a trump to the carefully preserved king in dummy. This draws the defenders' last trump and places you in dummy at the same time.

Play dummy's high heart discarding a club loser in your hand. You've made your contract, losing two diamonds and a heart.

What would have happened if you first drew all the trumps? You could start on the hearts, but all West has to do is hold off winning one round. He then keeps on playing diamonds until you ruff. You are effectively shut out of the dummy and cannot take advantage of the heart winners there. Eventually you must surrender a club to the opponents.

♦ ♦ ♦ ♦ ♦

## YOU NEED TRUMPS AS ENTRIES TO TAKE REPEATED FINESSES IN SIDE SUITS

Another set of circumstances where it is advisable to delay drawing trumps is when you need dummy's trumps as entries in order to take necessary finesses.

Let's try this hand:

| West | | | East |
|------|------|------|------|
| ♠ A 6 3 | | | ♠ 8 7 2 |
| ♥ K J 10 7 6 | | | ♥ A Q 9 |
| ♦ A J 10 9 | | | ♦ 6 5 2 |
| ♣ A | | | ♣ J 8 6 2 |

| Bidding: | West | North | East | South |
|----------|------|-------|------|-------|
| | 1♥ | 1♠ | 2♥ | Pass |
| | 4♥ | All Pass | | |

Opening Lead: ♠K

103

## PLANNING:

You have two sure losers in spades, two possible losers in diamonds and no losers in hearts or clubs.
There's nothing to be done about the spades.
How can you eliminate one loser in diamonds?
Are there discarding possibilities?
Are any finesses available?
Should you draw trumps immediately?

The Complete Hand:

Dealer: West

```
                    North
                    ♠ K Q J 10 4
                    ♥ 4 2
                    ♦ Q 4
                    ♣ K Q 10 9
    West                            East
    ♠ A 6 3                         ♠ 8 7 2
    ♥ K J 10 7 6                    ♥ A Q 9
    ♦ A J 10 9                      ♦ 6 5 2
    ♣ A                             ♣ J 8 6 2
                    South
                    ♠ 9 5
                    ♥ 8 5 3
                    ♦ K 8 7 3
                    ♣ 7 5 4 3
```

| Bidding: | West | North | East | South |
|----------|------|-------|------|-------|
|          | 1♥   | 1♠    | 2♥   | Pass  |
|          | 4♥   | All Pass |    |       |

Opening Lead: ♠K

## THE PLAY:

Win the opening lead with the ♠A. Your only chance of success is to attempt diamond finesses. For this to work you need entries to dummy. The vehicle is the trump suit.

Play a small trump to dummy's 9. Lead a small diamond and finesse with the 9, which loses to North's queen. North cashes the ♠Q J and switches to the ♣K.

You win the ace and play a small trump to dummy's queen. This enables you to lead another diamond toward your hand. When South plays small you finesse with the 10. This succeeds.

You play another trump to dummy's ace which draws the defender's last trump and places you in a position to take another finesse. You take another successful diamond "hook" and you bring your contract home.

You had all the percentages and odds on your side. The finesses had a 75% chance of success and the extra entries to dummy provided for the possible four-two break in the diamond suit.

♦ ♦ ♦ ♦ ♦

## DELAY DRAWING TRUMPS
## TO MAINTAIN CONTROL OF THE HAND

Sometimes, even when things look rosy, care must be taken about the timing of drawing all the opponents' trumps.

This hand illustrates this principle:

```
Dealer: North
                        North
                        ♠ 10 7 4
                        ♥ 6 5 3
                        ♦ K 6 2
                        ♣ A 7 4 3
        West                            East
        ♠ 2                             ♠ 9 8 6 5
        ♥ K Q J 10                      ♥ A 9 7 2
        ♦ A 10 9 3                      ♦ 8 7 4
        ♣ J 10 9 8                      ♣ 6 2
                        South
                        ♠ A K Q J 3
                        ♥ 8 4
                        ♦ Q J 5
                        ♣ K Q 5
```

| Bidding: | West | North | East | South |
|----------|------|-------|------|-------|
|          | ---- | Pass  | Pass | 1♠    |
|          | Dbl  | 2♠    | Pass | 4♠    |
|          | All Pass | | | |

Opening Lead: ♥K

The opponents win the first two heart tricks and you ruff the third. You do your planning and realize that you've lost two tricks and have another loser in diamonds. That looks like *it!* You've got solid trumps and clubs.

106

If you can safely draw the trumps you will give up a diamond to the ace and your Q J will be established.

You start drawing trumps. You play the jack and everybody follows. You play the queen and ----OOPS!----West shows out! That means that East has four spades, the same number you now have.

### STOP AND THINK!

1. If you play a third spade and then play diamonds, West will win and play another heart which you would have to ruff. But that would establish East's fourth spade as a trick. Result: Down one.

2. If you draw all four trumps, you still have to give up a diamond. West will win and cash a high heart. Result: Down one.

3. Stop, think . . . and stop drawing trumps at this point, while you still have a trump left in dummy. Give up a diamond trick to West's ace. Now, if a heart is played you can ruff it in dummy, discarding a minor suit card in your hand.

You reach your hand in either minor suit. At this point you can safely draw the balance of the trumps. The rest of your hand is high.

One tactic of the defense is to try to reduce declarer's trumps to fewer than one of the defenders. The methods we discussed in this hand are one way to counteract it. It is sometimes necessary to delay drawing trumps in order to retain trumps in dummy to help maintain control of the hand.

◆ ◆ ◆ ◆ ◆

## *A FEW SIDELIGHTS and TIDBITS:*

In the interest of simplicity we've been using the terms "dummy" and "declarer" while discussing the handling of the trump suit. It is a generalization, as the dummy usually has fewer trumps and the declarer the longer trumps. But there are many cases where the situation is reversed. In your mind just consider the "long hand" as the declarer and the "short hand" as the dummy.

♦ ♦ ♦ ♦ ♦

You may have noticed that when dummy has A K, we've suggested playing the king. Yes, it really makes no difference. But as people get older and memories get shorter, four or five tricks later it is comforting to know that you have the highest card in the suit and don't have to remember, "Was the ace already played or not?"

♦ ♦ ♦ ♦ ♦

In the many hands you will encounter, as you extend your bridge experience, you will be faced with a choice of plays.

Do you take a finesse or do you attempt to establish a suit? If you decide to set up a suit, which of two possible suits do you select?

A working knowledge of the probabilities of how suits will break can be helpful in making the winning decisions. The chart on the next page can act as a guide. You don't have to memorize it . . . but having a general awareness is a good idea.

## AN **ODD** NUMBER OF HIDDEN CARDS TEND TO DIVIDE *EVENLY!*

| NO. OF CARDS | DIVIDE: | PERCENT OF TIME* |
|---|---|---|
| **3** | 2-1 | 78. |
|  | 3-0 | 22. |
| **5** | 3-2 | 68. |
|  | 4-1 | 28. |
|  | 5-0 | 4. |
| **7** | 4-3 | 62. |
|  | 5-2 | 31. |
|  | 6-1 | 7. |
|  | 7-0 | 1. |

## AN **EVEN** NUMBER OF HIDDEN CARDS TEND TO DIVIDE *UNEVENLY!*

| NO. OF CARDS | DIVIDE: | PERCENT OF TIME* |
|---|---|---|
| **2** | 1-1 | 52. |
|  | 2-0 | 48. |
| **4** | 3-1 | 50. |
|  | 2-2 | 41. |
|  | 4-0 | 10. |
| **6** | 4-2 | 48. |
|  | 3-3 | 36. |
|  | 5-1 | 15. |
|  | 6-0 | 1. |

A GUIDE TO THE POSSIBLE DIVISIONS OF OUTSTANDING CARDS WHEN PLAYING A SUIT. YOU DON'T HAVE TO MEMORIZE IT... *JUST REMEMBER*... ODD NUMBER OF OUTSTANDING CARDS TEND TO DIVIDE EVENLY, AN EVEN NUMBER, UNEVENLY.       *ROUNDED TO NEAREST PERCENT.

# CHAPTER 6

# DECLARER PLAY IN NOTRUMP CONTRACTS

*Planning the Play*

♦ ♦ ♦ ♦

*How to Count Winners*

♦ ♦ ♦ ♦

*How to Develop
Additional Tricks Safely*

♦ ♦ ♦ ♦

*The Hold-up Play*

♦ ♦ ♦ ♦

*Keeping the Dangerous Hand
Out of the Lead*

♦ ♦ ♦ ♦

*Maintaining Communications*

The get-rich-quick road to game is three notrump. It requires only nine tricks while suit contracts require ten or eleven.

Quickest, however, is not necessarily easiest. In notrump you do not have the luxury of being able to trump opponents' high cards. The guidelines for determining the strategy of declarer play is therefore different.

### THE PLANNING

As in a suit contract, we have to proceed with a plan in notrump . . . but the plan has to be different.

In suit contract planning we generally start out by counting losers. In notrump we count winners. What is the use of counting losers in one suit, when the opponents can run many tricks in another?

When you hold ♦K Q J 10 9, it contains only one loser. But of what significance is it, if upon obtaining the lead with their ♦A the opponents can run ♣A K Q J 10?

Notrump planning starts with: How many sure tricks do you have, "off-the-top," before relinquishing the lead to the opponents? When do you start the planning? *Before* you play dummy's first card.

The accompanying chart indicates the areas to consider in establishing your plan of action.

1. How many tricks do I have "off-the-top?"
2. If it is not sufficient to fulfill my contract, how can I develop additional tricks safely?
3. Which suit do I play?
4. Are there any finesses to take?
5. Should I win the first trick if I can, or should I hold up one or more rounds?
6. Is there a "dangerous hand" that I can prevent from obtaining the lead?
7. Do I have sufficient entries to carry out my plan?

**NOTRUMP PLANNING** STARTS WITH A POSITIVE ATTITUDE. *YOU COUNT WINNERS!*

1. HOW MANY WINNERS DO YOU HAVE *"OFF-THE TOP?"*

2. HOW DO YOU DEVELOP ADDITIONAL TRICKS, SAFELY?

3. DO YOU WIN THE FIRST TRICK, OR *DO YOU HOLD UP?*

4. WHICH SUIT DO YOU PLAY FIRST?

5. ARE THERE ANY FINESSES?

6. IS THERE A DANGEROUS HAND?

7. DO YOU WIN IN DUMMY OR IN YOUR HAND? WATCH FOR ENTRIES.

## COUNTING WINNERS

In the following hands you are in a 3NT contract:
A.    How many tricks do you have "off-the-top"
B.    How many additional tricks do you need?
C.    Which suit do you go after first?  Why?

Example 1:

```
                          Dummy
                          North
                          ♠A 3 2
                          ♥K 6 2
                          ♦5 3
                          ♣Q J 9 8 3


                          You
                          South
                          ♠K 7 6
                          ♥A Q 8
                          ♦K Q 8 4
                          ♣K 6 4
Opening Lead:  ♠Q
```

Example 1:
A.    You have five tricks: Two spades and three hearts.
B.    You need four more.
C.    Clubs seems like your best bet.  Lead small to the queen, then back to your king.  If they break 3-2 your hand is made.  If they break 4-1, you still can make four tricks if left hand opponent has the four cards.  You have a proven finesse against his 10.

Example 2:

```
                          Dummy
                          North
                          ♠ A 5
                          ♥ 10 8 5
                          ♦ A J 10 9 2
                          ♣ J 10 3

                          You
                          South
                          ♠ K 10 2
                          ♥ A K 9 2
                          ♦ Q 6 3
                          ♣ A 9 5
Opening Lead:  ♣4
```

Example 2:

A.  You have six tricks: Two spades, two hearts, plus one each
    in diamonds and clubs.

B.  You need three more tricks.

C.  Go after the diamond suit first. Lead the ♦Q and attempt
    a finesse. If the finesse loses, the defense will cash their
    club trick and put you back in the lead with another club.
    The diamond suit is established and you can run 10 tricks
    Of course, if the finesse wins you will bag 11 tricks.

Example 3:

```
                        Dummy
                        North
                        ♠ J 8
                        ♥ 7 6 5
                        ♦ K 9 3
                        ♣ A Q 10 4 2

                        You
                        South
                        ♠ K Q 10 2
                        ♥ A Q J
                        ♦ A 10 8
                        ♣ J 9 3
Opening Lead:  ♥3
```

Example 3:

A. You have five tricks. Two hearts, two diamonds and one club.
B. You need four more tricks.
C. In the two previous examples, the selection of the correct suit to work on first was relatively easy. One suit in each case stood out quite clearly

In example 3, however, there are two suits vying for consideration, spades and clubs. Which do you select, and why?

### SELECTING THE PROPER SUIT TO PLAY
The order in which suits are played is even more critical in notrump than in suit contracts.

You can have lots of high-card points, much more than may be required for a 3NT contract, and be devastated by the wrong defender obtaining the lead at the wrong time.

116

Examine the complete hand:

```
                    North
                    ♠ J 8
                    ♥ 7 6 5
                    ♦ K 9 3
                    ♣ A Q 10 4 2
    West                            East
    ♠ A 7 6                         ♠ 9 5 4 3
    ♥ K 10 8 3 2                    ♥ 9 4
    ♦ 7 5 2                         ♦ Q J 6 4
    ♣ 7 6                           ♣ K 8 5
                    South
                    ♠ K Q 10 2
                    ♥ A Q J
                    ♦ A 10 8
                    ♣ J 9 3
```

| Bidding: | West | North | East | South |
|----------|------|-------|------|-------|
|          | —    | Pass  | Pass | 1 NT  |
|          | Pass | 3 NT  | All Pass |   |

Opening Lead: ♥3

The heart lead is won by your jack. You are faced with the choice of embarking on establishing either the club or spade suit.

The "obvious" suit to begin with seems to be clubs. If the finesse is successful, you have all the tricks you need.

But what happens if it is not successful?

In the hand, as shown, East wins the ♣K and returns a heart. You finesse with the queen and West wins the trick. He continues another heart which establishes the balance of the suit, as you win the ace.

117

At this point you have only eight available tricks. You must attempt to establish an additional trick in the spade suit. West, however, holds the ace. Upon obtaining the lead, West will be able to run two additional heart tricks to defeat the contract.

The importance of *first* playing a suit that removes West's possible entry comes strongly into focus. West's opening lead indicates a possible five-card suit. Your job is to prevent West from establishing the suit. Or failing that, making sure that he does not obtain the lead if it does get established.

By playing the spade suit first, you, as declarer, have all options open to you. It is guaranteed to give you three tricks. If West wins the ♠A, he cannot effectively attack the heart suit because he would be playing into your A Q  He may switch to a diamond which you  win. You take the club finesse which loses to East's king.

When he returns a heart, hop up with your ace. You now run all your established tricks. You've lost only one spade and one club, making 5NT.

If East has the ♠A, he will undoubtedly attack your hearts. You finesse with the queen which you most likely lose to West's king. You win the heart return.

You attempt the club finesse. Though, in this case, it loses to East, he is now void of hearts. He cannot play the suit to West. East is forced to play one of your suits. Your hand is now all set up and you run all your winners, making ten tricks. You've lost one spade, one heart and one club.

By playing spades first, you make your contract regardless of the distribution.

By playing clubs first, you succeed only when the finesse succeeds

The clue to successful notrump play is to try to establish tricks *safely*.

## THE HOLD-UP PLAY

When the defense makes their opening lead, this decision often faces the declarer, "Do I win the opening trick or do I hold off for one or more rounds?"

What is the reason for refraining from winning the opponent's lead?

Here's how the hold-up play is supposed to work:

1. The defense leads their best suit.
2. You hold off winning until one of the defenders is out of the suit.
3. Play the hand in such a way that only the void defender obtains the lead.
4. That defender is thus unable to play the suit again, even though it may have been established.

Example:

```
        West                    East
      ♠ A 6 5                 ♠ 9 2
      ♥ K 8 5                 ♥ A Q 3
      ♦ A 10 9 8 3            ♦ Q J 7
      ♣ 9 3                   ♣ A K J 10 5
  Contract: 3NT by East
  Opening Lead: ♠K
```

## THE PLANNING

1.  How many tricks do you have "off-the-top?"

2.  How many additional tricks do you need?

3.  Where can you obtain them?

4.  Should you win the opening lead, or hold up?
    If you should hold up, for how many rounds?

5.  Which suit should you attack?  Why?

The complete hand:

| | North | |
| --- | --- | --- |
| | ♠ 7 4 3 | |
| | ♥ J 10 6 4 | |
| | ♦ K 6 4 | |
| | ♣ 6 4 2 | |

| West | | East |
| --- | --- | --- |
| ♠ A 6 5 | | ♠ 9 2 |
| ♥ K 8 5 | | ♥ A Q 3 |
| ♦ A 10 9 8 3 | | ♦ Q J 7 |
| ♣ 9 3 | | ♣ A K J 10 5 |

| | South | |
| --- | --- | --- |
| | ♠ K Q J 10 8 | |
| | ♥ 9 7 2 | |
| | ♦ 5 2 | |
| | ♣ Q 8 7 | |

Bidding:

| | West | North | East | South |
| --- | --- | --- | --- | --- |
| | --- | --- | 1NT | Pass |
| | 3NT | All Pass | | |

Opening Lead: ♠K

## THE PLAY

1. You have seven tricks available.
2. You need two additional tricks.
3. You have two choices, the diamond or club suit.
4. You can afford to hold up. If the opening leader has a five-card spade suit, his partner holds only three spades. You can hold up until the third round.
5. Either clubs and diamonds can provide the two additional tricks you need. Each suit requires a finesse. If you win, either suit is fine. But what happens if the finesse loses?

121

If the club finesse loses, South obtains the lead and can run the established spade suit to defeat the contract.

If the diamond finesse loses, North is in the lead. However, because of the hold-up play, he no longer has any spades. He must put you back into the lead and you make your contract with an overtrick.

The actual play would go something like this:

You hold off winning the spade leads until the third round, discarding a small club on the third spade.

Reach your hand with a heart to your queen, and take the diamond finesse by leading the ♦Q. North wins the ♦K. Having no spades to play, he leads a small club, hoping his partner holds the ace. But his wishes are in vain, you hold the A K. You do not take any club finesses and run the balance of high cards making ten tricks.

When you consider when to hold up, you should also decide when *not* to hold up. Here are some guidelines.

### *DO NOT HOLD UP IF:*
1. You can run sufficient tricks for your contract.

2. The opponents can switch to another suit that may be more dangerous.

3. You may lose your trick and control of the suit, if you don't take the trick immediately.

Example 1.

```
                        Dummy
                        ♠ Q 8 5
                        ♥ A 9
                        ♦ Q 4 3
                        ♣ J 6 4 3 2

                        You
                        ♠ 7 3
                        ♥ J 6 3
                        ♦ A K 5 2
                        ♣ A K Q 7
Contract:  3NT
Opening Lead:  ♥K
```

Take your ace. You have nine tricks. Do not fool around.

Example 2.

```
                        Dummy
                        ♠ 7 2
                        ♥ 9 5 4 2
                        ♦ K Q J 9 4
                        ♣ K 3

                        You
                        ♠ K 5 4
                        ♥ A 10
                        ♦ A 7 6 5
                        ♣ A J 9 5
Contract:  3NT
Opening Lead:  ♥6
```

On the ♥6 lead, your right-hand opponent plays the ♥Q.

Take the ace. Dummy's 9 may stand up as a trick if the suit is played eventually. If you hold up, a small card will force your ace and the opponents' K J will provide two or three additional tricks.

But even more important, your right hand defender may switch to a ♠Q, attacking your ♠K. If your left hand opponent holds the ♠A, you can quickly lose three or more tricks in the suit.

Example 3.

```
                    Dummy
                    ♠ A Q 5
                    ♥ 8 7 6
                    ♦ K Q 6 4
                    ♣ 9 8 3

                    You
                    ♠ K 9 8 2
                    ♥ K 10 3
                    ♦ A 10 3
                    ♣ A Q 10

Contract: 3NT
Opening Lead: ♥5
```

On the ♥5 opening lead your right hand opponent plays the queen. Take the king. If you do not, he can continue hearts through your king, permitting his partner to run a five-card suit.

The opponents' hands may be distributed something like this:

♥A J 9 5 2                    ♥Q 4

124

## KEEPING THE DANGEROUS HAND OUT OF THE LEAD

Although neither of the opponents goes out of the way to help you, many times one of the opponents is more dangerous than the other.

DANGEROUS DIANA

SAFETY SAMANTHA

*H·L.*

Throughout the discussions on notrump play, developing tricks *safely* has been emphasized. The hold-up play is one example of the lengths declarer has to go to establish tricks safely. Preventing the "dangerous opponent" from obtaining the lead at a time that is disadvantageous to the declarer is an important tactic, particularly in notrump. The fancy name for this maneuver is, "The Avoidance Play."

Depending on the circumstances, sometimes it is the opening leader, sometimes it is the other defender. Careful attention to the bidding and play will often supply the clues.

Example 1.

| | You | | Dummy | |
|---|---|---|---|---|
| | West | | East | |
| | ♠ A K | | ♠ 8 5 3 | |
| | ♥ 9 8 2 | | ♥ K 3 | |
| | ♦ A J 10 4 | | ♦ K 9 8 3 2 | |
| | ♣ K Q 10 9 | | ♣ A 8 4 | |
| Bidding: | West | North | East | South |
| | --- | --- | --- | Pass |
| | 1 NT | Pass | 3 NT | All Pass |
| Opening Lead : ♠Q | | | | |

125

This example brings the principle of the avoidance play clearly into focus.

In your planning, you can count seven tricks without relinquishing the lead. You need two additional tricks. The fairly obvious suit to obtain these tricks is diamonds.

There are, however, three ways to go. You can play for the outstanding queen to drop, or you can finesse either way. Which method do you choose?

The principle of avoiding the dangerous defender dictates the choice. Bromides such as, "Nine-never, eight-ever," go out the window in face of the realities of the situation.

What is your concern in this particular hand? Is there a dangerous defender? If so, which one?

Your concern is: If a defender obtains the lead, your heart suit will be attacked. If North gets the lead, a heart switch through dummy's king may easily defeat the contract.

If, however, South is on lead, he cannot effectively attack the heart suit without permitting dummy to win a trick with the ♥K. The answer to this problem is to play the diamond suit so that North cannot obtain the lead.

Playing for the drop may not work as North may hold three diamonds to the queen. The only sure way to make the contract is for declarer to take a diamond finesse through North.

The procedure is: Declarer plays the ♦A. If the queen doesn't drop singleton, continue with the ♦J. If North doesn't cover, let it ride. Even if it loses to South, your diamond tricks are established and ♥K remains in a position to stop the suit.

The Complete Hand:

```
Dealer: South
                        North
                        ♠ Q J 10 9 7
                        ♥ 10 7 4
                        ♦ Q 7 5
                        ♣ 3 2
        West                            East
        ♠ A K                           ♠ 8 5 3
        ♥ 9 8 2                         ♥ K 3
        ♦ A J 10 4                      ♦ K 9 8 3 2
        ♣ K Q 10 9                      ♣ A 8 4
                        South
                        ♠ 6 4 2
                        ♥ A Q J 6 5
                        ♦ 6
                        ♣ J 7 6 5
```

| Bidding: | West | North | East | South |
|----------|------|-------|------|-------|
|          | —    | —     | —    | Pass  |
|          | 1 NT | Pass  | 3 NT | All Pass |

Opening Lead: ♠Q

In this hand North, the opening leader, is the dangerous hand. An attempt to drop the ♦Q would have been unsuccessful. North, upon obtaining the lead, would switch to hearts and the hand would be defeated. The correct play, finessing through the North hand, pays an extra bonus in providing overtricks when the queen is onside. The point of the play is that the contract was secured even if the finesse lost.

Example 2.

<table>
<tr><td colspan="4">You</td></tr>
<tr><td colspan="4">North</td></tr>
<tr><td colspan="4">♠ J 8 3</td></tr>
<tr><td colspan="4">♥ A K 7</td></tr>
<tr><td colspan="4">♦ A Q 10</td></tr>
<tr><td colspan="4">♣ K 10 9 7</td></tr>
<tr><td colspan="4">Dummy</td></tr>
<tr><td colspan="4">South</td></tr>
<tr><td colspan="4">♠ A 6</td></tr>
<tr><td colspan="4">♥ Q 8 5 4</td></tr>
<tr><td colspan="4">♦ J 9 6</td></tr>
<tr><td colspan="4">♣ A J 6 5</td></tr>
</table>

| Bidding: | West | North | East | South |
|---|---|---|---|---|
|  | Pass | 1 NT | Pass | 3 NT |
|  | All Pass |  |  |  |

Opening Lead: ♠K

As the ♠K is led you ponder this hand.

Off-the-top, you have seven tricks, you need only two more. You have finesse possibilities in diamonds and clubs.

Three decisions face you at this moment.

1. Should you win the first trick or hold up?
2. Is there a dangerous hand? Opening leader or his partner?
3. Which suit do you go after first? If it's clubs which way do you finesse?

1. If you hold up, you will lose the potential stopper of the ♠J in your hand. The defender will simply continue with a small spade suit knocking out dummy's ace. The opening leader has established the spade suit and his partner may have a third spade to reach him in the event he obtains the lead. It would make no difference which defender gets the lead. Do not hold up. Win the opening lead with the ace.

128

2. Now that you've won ♠A, you've exposed your ♠J to possible capture...if the wrong hand obtains the lead. Who's the dangerous defender? This time it's West, the opening leader's partner.
3. In this instance you have to protect your ♠J from attack. You have to plan your play so that West does not obtain the lead prematurely. Play the club suit by finessing through West.

The Complete Hand:

```
Dealer: South
                              You
                              North
                              ♠ J 8 3
                              ♥ A K 7
                              ♦ A Q 10
                              ♣ K 10 9 7

      West                                      East
      ♠ 7 4 2                                   ♠ K Q 10 9 5
      ♥ J 10 6 2                                ♥ 9 3
      ♦ 7 5 4 3                                 ♦ K 8 2
      ♣ 8 3                                     ♣ Q 4 2

                              Dummy
                              South
                              ♠ A 6
                              ♥ Q 8 5 4
                              ♦ J 9 6
                              ♣ A J 6 5
```

| Bidding: | West | North | East | South |
|---|---|---|---|---|
| | Pass | 1 NT | Pass | 3 NT |
| | All Pass | | | |

Opening Lead: ♠K

129

After winning the opening lead with dummy's ♠A, you go after the club suit, attempting to keep West off lead.

Play the ♣A, followed by the jack. When this loses to East's queen, he cannot play a spade without establishing dummy's jack as the ninth trick.

If East makes a passive lead, either a club or a heart, you win it in your hand. Cash your club winners and the hearts winding up in dummy with the ♥Q.

When the hearts don't break evenly, you attempt the diamond finesse by playing the ♦J. It loses to East's king. Again, East cannot play spades without giving you an extra trick. East, therefore, returns a diamond, but you have your nine tricks. Although in this case both finesses lost, you've played in such a way that the success of your contract was guaranteed.

♦ ♦ ♦ ♦ ♦

## MAINTAINING ENTRIES
## AND LINES OF COMMUNICATIONS

A common error of less experienced players is to fail to recognize the interrelations of different suits in the play of the hand.

Have you ever seen some declarers who feel so elated about winning tricks that they gobble up some easy side suit winners before they go about the business of *developing* winners?

Take a look at this happy-go-lucky declarer as he plays this solid 3NT contract.

130

When East played the ♥Q on the opening lead, this declarer won the ace and did a quick calculation. He already had one heart trick in the bank, plus four sure diamond tricks. And after taking a club finesse, even if it loses, four additional club tricks. That makes nine tricks. There are even a few extra tricks possibilities in spades and hearts.

So our delightful declarer went about the happy task of cashing the ♦A K Q J.

Then he started on clubs. He led the ♣J, and happily it won. He led another club to dummy's 10, and unhappily it lost to East's king.

East returned a heart to his partner's ♥K. West continued the suit, declarer winning with his ♥10.

This is how declarer's assets looked at that moment:

```
                    Dummy
                    North
                    ♠ 9
                    ♥ ---
                    ♦ ---
                    ♣ A Q 9


                    Declarer
                    South
                    ♠ K Q 7 2
                    ♥ ---
                    ♦ ---
                    ♣ —
```

He had seven tricks in the bank, four diamonds, two hearts, and one club.

His *real* assets were ♠K Q in his hand, but the ♣A Q 9 in dummy were *frozen* assets.

He had no choice but to play the ♠K, which West won and ran his two set-up heart tricks. Declarer eventually won his ♠Q, but the contract was defeated because he had lost three hearts, one club and one spade.

This is the complete hand:

```
Dealer: North
                        North
                        ♠ 9 6
                        ♥ 8 5
                        ♦ A 6 5 4
                        ♣ A Q 10 9 3
        West                            East
        ♠ A 3                           ♠ J 10 8 5 4
        ♥ K 9 7 6 2                     ♥ Q 4 3
        ♦ 10 9 7                        ♦ 3 2
        ♣ 6 5 2                         ♣ K 8 7
                        South
                        ♠ K Q 7 2
                        ♥ A J 10
                        ♦ K Q J 8
                        ♣ J 4
```

Contract: 3 NT by South
Opening Lead: ♥6

In his "planning" this declarer neglected one vital aspect. He didn't see the relationship between the diamond and club suits.

In order for the club suit to become effective, an entry to dummy in the diamond suit had to be retained.

The proper play, therefore, is to start playing the club suit at trick two. No matter how the defenders play, declarer must make at least 10 tricks.

One reason declarers continually make similar mistakes is that they often get away with these blunders because some defenders are not astute enough to refuse to win the first club trick. As a result the declarer often makes the contract, completely unaware of the error he committed.

Sound declarer play requires planning, foresight and attention to detail.

133

# SOME ADVANCED TECHNIQUES IN DECLARER PLAY

### *The Strip and End Play*
♦ ♦ ♦ ♦
### *The Simple Squeeze*
♦ ♦ ♦ ♦
### *Deceptive Play*
♦ ♦ ♦ ♦
### *Dummy Reversal*
♦ ♦ ♦ ♦

## THE STRIP & END PLAY

Life is funny and so is bridge. No sooner have you learned how to do something, when someone tells you how to avoid doing it.

You've learned all about finesses: Simple and double finesses, two-way finesses, deep finesses and ruffing finesses. You know that they're all percentage plays, usually 75%, 50% or 25%.

Now we come along and suggest the possibility of using the Strip & End Play technique to convert a percentage play into what is often a "sure thing."

As the opportunity to execute a Strip & End Play comes up quite often, it should be in the arsenal of all good players. The method is to *strip* the opponents of key suits so they do not have a safe exit from their hands. Then put them into the lead. They *end* up having to make an advantageous lead to you.

The key is to recognize the conditions when using the *strip & end play* is feasible.

## 1. *Avoiding a Guess in a Two-Way Finesse Situation* .

> *Dummy:* A J 7
> *You:* K 10 3

You'd want to avoid like a plague making a guess in this setup..
Look for the *Strip & End Play* possibility.
You've arrived at a 6 ♥ contract. The opening lead is the ♣ K.

| Dummy | You |
|-------|-----|
| ♠ A J 7 | ♠ K 10 3 |
| ♥ Q J 9 5 2 | ♥ A K 10 6 3 |
| ♦ A Q 7 | ♦ K 8 6 |
| ♣ A 3 | ♣ 6 5 |

Your slam contract is sound, but you do have a sure club loser
and a possible spade loser. You can take a stab at guessing who
has the ♠Q, or you can let the *strip & end play* come to the
rescue.

Win the opening lead, draw trumps, play three rounds of
diamonds, stripping your hands of the suit. You arrive at this
setup:

| Dummy | You |
|-------|-----|
| ♠ A J 7 | ♠ K 10 3 |
| ♥ J 9 5 | ♥ K 10 6 |
| ♦ — | ♦ — |
| ♣ 3 | ♣ 6 |

Now play your last club which completes the *stripping* part of
the play. Either opponent *ends* up on lead with no winning
choice. A spade return gives you a free finesse, while a diamond
or club play permits a ruff in one hand and a sluff of a spade in
the other hand.

The Complete Hand:

```
                        North
                        ♠ A J 7
                        ♥ Q J 9 5 2
                        ♦ A Q 7
                        ♣ A 3
West                                        East
♠ 9 6 4                                     ♠ Q 8 5 2
♥ 8 4                                       ♥ 7
♦ J 9 4                                     ♦ 10 5 3 2
♣ K Q J 9 4                                 ♣ 10 8 7 2
                        South
                        ♠ K 10 3
                        ♥ A K 10 6 3
                        ♦ K 8 6
                        ♣ 6 5
```

Contract: 6♥ by South
Opening Lead: ♣ K

The Strip and End Play guaranteed your contract.

Another card combination where you would prefer to have the opponents lead the suit for you is:
J 6 3 opposite Q 7 5.

With this setup try to use the strip and end play whenever possible. Let the opponents lead the suit for you.

## 2. *"Loser-on-a-Loser" Technique*

```
Dummy              You
♠ 6 3 2            ♠ A Q 4
♥ A J 3            ♥ 2
♦ K J 10 8 5       ♦ A Q 9 6 4
♣ 7 4             ♣ A K 6 5
```

Despite a 2 ♥ overcall you arrive at a 6 ♦ contract.
The opening lead: ♥ K.

In planning the hand, you start out with four possible losers:
two clubs and two spades. You can ruff the two clubs in dummy.
But what about the two spades? With a successful finesse, a
50% chance, you can bring home the contract. Is there a better
way? Let's try the strip and end play, with the loser-on-a-loser
technique.

Draw trumps in two rounds. Play ♣ A K and ruff the third
club in dummy. Here comes the first key play: Return to your
hand by ruffing the ♥3. Reenter dummy by ruffing your last
club.

```
You've reached this position:
Dummy              You
♠ 6 3 2            ♠ A Q 4
♥ J                ♥ ---
♦ J                ♦ Q 9
♣ —               ♣ —
```

Now the second key play: Play the ♥J and *discard* the ♠4 from your hand . . . *the loser-on-a-loser play.* You've stripped your hands of both clubs and hearts.

South is now on lead. He must either play into your ♠A Q or lead a club or a diamond giving you a ruff in dummy and a spade discard in your hand. Your 50% chance has been converted into a 100% sure thing. South's heart bid as well as his ♥K lead virtually guaranteed that he held the ♥Q. You, therefore, were putting him into the lead with a "known card."

The complete hand:

North
♠ J 9 7 5
♥ 7 5 4
♦ 3 2
♣ J 9 3 2

*Dummy*
West
♠ 6 3 2
♥ A J 3
♦ K J 10 8 5
♣ 7 4

*You*
East
♠ A Q 4
♥ 2
♦ A Q 9 6 4
♣ A K 6 5

South
♠ K 10 8
♥ K Q 10 9 7 6
♦ 7
♣ Q 10 8

| Bidding: | West | North | East | South |
|---|---|---|---|---|
| | --- | — | 1 ♦ | 1 ♥ |
| | 3 ♦ | Pass | 4 ♣ | Pass |
| | 4 ♥ | Pass | 4 NT | Pass |
| | 5 ♦ | Pass | 6 ♦ | All Pass |
| Opening Lead: ♥K | | | | |

140

## Avoiding a finesse by "Ducking."

```
                Dummy
                ♠ A K 4
                ♥ Q 10 7 4
                ♦ 8 7 3
                ♣ 7 6 3

                You
                ♠ Q 7 6
                ♥ A K J 6 3
                ♦ 6 2
                ♣ A Q 9
```

Depending upon styles, bidding may take several routes. You, South, as dealer may open the bidding with either 1♥ or 1 NT.

| 1. West | North | East | South |
|---------|-------|------|-------|
| --- | --- | --- | 1 ♥ |
| Dbl. | 2 ♥ | Pass | 3 ♣ |
| 3 ♦ | 4 ♥ | All Pass | |

| 2. West | North | East | South |
|---------|-------|------|-------|
| --- | --- | -— | 1 ♥ |
| 2 ♦ | 2 ♥ | Pass | 3 ♣ |
| Pass | 4 ♥ | All Pass | |

| 3. West | North | East | South |
|---------|-------|------|-------|
| --- | --- | --- | 1 NT |
| 2 ♦ | 3 ♦* | Pass | 3 ♥ |
| Pass | 4 ♥ | All Pass | |
| *Stayman | | | |

In any case, West will compete. But eventually you wind up in a 4♥ contract. Opening lead: ♦A or ♦K (depending on style).

141

In planning the play, declarer can count two sure diamond losers and two *possible* club losers. Two club losers are one too many for the contract to succeed. A successful finesse may be a way to eliminate one loser. But based on the bidding, West is very likely to have the ♣K. Perhaps there is a better way. Let's try *The Strip & End Play.*

After ruffing the third round of diamonds, declarer draws trumps in two or three rounds. The *stripping* process is completed by playing all the spades, being careful to wind up in dummy, which leaves this position:

| Dummy | Declarer |
|---|---|
| ♠ — | ♠ — |
| ♥ 10 | ♥ J |
| ♦ – | ♦ — |
| ♣ 7 6 3 | ♣ A Q 9 |

A small club is played from dummy. If East plays small*, play the nine. This *ends* up placing West in the lead. He must play a club into your ace-queen, or lead a spade or a diamond, which permits a ruff in one hand and a club discard in the other.

The Complete Hand:  North *Dummy*

> ♠ A K 4
> ♥ Q 10 7 4
> ♦ 8 7 3
> ♣ 7 6 3

West
♠ J 9 5 2
♥ 9
♦ A K Q 10 5
♣ K J 8

East
♠ 10 8 3
♥ 8 5 2
♦ J 9 4
♣ 10 5 4 2

> South *You*
> ♠ Q 7 6
> ♥ A K J 6 3
> ♦ 6 2
> ♣ A Q 9

*When the clubs are played, if East plays either a jack or ten, you cover with your queen, making your ace-nine a tenace position. (A little defensive note: Whenever you are in the same position as East, do not automatically play "second hand low." Insert a high card, such as a jack or ten. If declarer doesn't hold the nine, you can thwart the "ducking aspect" of the end play.)

### *Half a loaf is better than none.*

Many *Strip and End Play* hands convert a 50% chance into a sure thing. But we're not always so lucky. Here's a hand where you may convert a sure *failure* into a 50% chance of success.

You've arrived at a 6♣ contract after West interfered with a heart bid along the way.

This is what you face after a ♥K opening lead by West.

```
        Dummy
        North
        ♠ Q 3
        ♥ A J
        ♦ K J 7 5
        ♣ Q 10 6 3 2


        You
        South
        ♠ A 6
        ♥ 8 6
        ♦ A Q 6 4
        ♣ A K J 7 4
```

It looks like a reasonable contract with all four aces and 31 high card points between you. But you suffer from a mirror-image distribution with no possibility for a discard of a loser. You have only 11 tricks available off the top. The *Strip and End Play* is your only hope.

You win the ♥A, draw all the opponents' trumps and cash all the diamonds, which leaves this situation:

Dummy

♠ Q 3
♥ J
♦ —
♣ 10 6

You

♠ A 6
♥ 8
♦ —
♣ J 7

You are now at the moment of truth. You hope (a reasonable hope) that the opponent with the ♥Q also holds the ♠K. You play the ♥J, which completes the *stripping* and *ends* up placing a defender in the lead.

The end position of all four hands:

Dummy

♠ Q 3
♥ —
♦ —
♣ 10 6

West

♠ K 9 7
♥ 10
♦ —
♣ —

East

♠ J 10 8
♥ 3
♦ —
♣ —

You

♠ A 6
♥ —
♦ —
♣ J 7

West is now on lead. If a small spade is led, you hop up with dummy's queen and hope it wins. The king is in the West hand and you make your contract. Of course, if a heart is led you get a ruff in one hand and a spade discard in the other.

The Complete Hand:

North
♠ Q 3
♥ A J
♦ K J 7 5
♣ Q 10 6 3 2

West
♠ K 9 7 2
♥ K Q 10 9 7 5
♦ 10 8 2
♣ —

East
♠ J 10 8 5 4
♥ 4 3 2
♦ 9 3
♣ 9 8 5

South
♠ A 6
♥ 8 6
♦ A Q 6 4
♣ A K J 7 4

| The Bidding: | WEST | NORTH | EAST | SOUTH |
|---|---|---|---|---|
| | — | — | --- | 1 ♣ |
| | 2 ♥ | 3 ♥ | Pass | 4 ♦ |
| | Pass | 4 ♥ | Pass | 4 ♠ |
| | Pass | 6 ♣ | All Pass | |

Bidding a slam contract despite interference is one thing. Making it is another. Having the tools and the awareness of when and how to use them will reap rewards in the play.

♦ ♦ ♦ ♦

145

This tactic works in notrump contracts as well as in suit contracts. The big difference is that you do not have the luxury of a trump suit as a stopper. Hence, there are no *ruff and sluff* possibilities.

*Dummy*

North

♠ 7 4 3

♥ 8 7 6

♦ A J 6

♣ K Q J 4

*You*

South

♠ A 8 5 2

♥ A Q

♦ K 10 7

♣ A 7 6 5

In this example, you arrive at a 3 NT contract and receive the ♠K opening lead.

In planning the hand you count eight winners available without relinquishing the lead. You need one more trick to fulfill your contract. That extra trick may be possible by the *favorable* location of the defenders' honors in hearts or diamonds.

At this point, however, it is wise to hold up winning the ♠A to determine the distribution of the suit. West continues with the ♠Q and you win the third round play of the ♠J, as East shows out. You now know that West started with four spades.

You, at this point, can try to employ the strip and end play to avoid having to guess the location of the heart and diamond honors. Cash your four club winners, making sure to wind up in your hand. This strips West of the club suit.

This is now the situation:

| | Dummy | |
|---|---|---|
| | North | |
| | ♠ — | |
| | ♥ 8 7 6 | |
| | ♦ A J 6 | |
| | ♣ — | |

| West | | East |
|---|---|---|
| ♠ 9 | | ♠ — |
| ♥ K 9 | | ♥ J 10 5 |
| ♦ 9 7 5 | | ♦ Q 8 4 |
| ♣ — | | ♣--- |

| | You | |
|---|---|---|
| | South | |
| | ♠ 8 | |
| | ♥ A Q | |
| | ♦ K 10 7 | |
| | ♣ — | |

Play the ♠8 from your hand, discarding a small heart from dummy, which puts West into the lead. West is now *end-played.* He must play a diamond or a heart (that's all he's got) and your contract is assured. Actually, you also have a safe chance for an overtrick by taking a finesse in the suit that was not led.

Keep on the lookout for end-play possibilities. They'll save you tricks and help bring home many otherwise unmakable contracts

The complete hand is on the following page.

North
♠ 7 4 3
♥ 8 7 6
♦ A J 6
♣ K Q J 4

West
♠ K Q J 9
♥ K 9 4
♦ 9 7 5 3
♣ 9 3

East
♠ 10 8
♥ J 10 5 3 2
♦ Q 8 4
♣ 10 8 2

South
♠ A 6 5 2
♥ A Q
♦ K 10 7
♣ A 7 6 5

♦ ♦ ♦ ♦

## THE "SIMPLE" SQUEEZE

A great maneuver in bridge as well as baseball is *The Squeeze Play.* Sometimes you find yourself one trick short of fulfilling your contract. A finesse may not be available or indications are that it will not be successful. There are no strip and end play possibilities. Knowing how to execute a simple squeeze can come to the rescue.

The conditions required are:
1. You should be able to win all the remaining tricks except one.
2. An opponent has to protect a key card in two suits.
3. Your side holds a "threat" or "menace" card in these suits.
4. You hold a winner in a third suit "the squeeze card," which forces the opponent to make a losing discard.
5. In the end position you have entry to the proper hand to benefit from the squeeze.

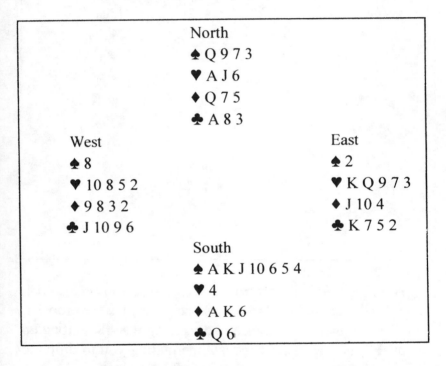

North
♠ Q 9 7 3
♥ A J 6
♦ Q 7 5
♣ A 8 3

West
♠ 8
♥ 10 8 5 2
♦ 9 8 3 2
♣ J 10 9 6

East
♠ 2
♥ K Q 9 7 3
♦ J 10 4
♣ K 7 5 2

South
♠ A K J 10 6 5 4
♥ 4
♦ A K 6
♣ Q 6

You wind up in an optimistic 7 ♠ contract and West leads the ♣J. You count 12 tricks available off the top. You feel that West would not have led from a king-jack combination against a grand slam contract, so you hop up with the ace. The only chance is a squeeze against East in the heart and club suits.

You play the ♠Q which draws the opponents' trumps and cash your three diamond tricks

You play all your trumps except one and arrive at this position:

```
                       Dummy
                       North
                       ♠ —
                       ♥ A J
                       ♦ —
                       ♣ 8

West                                    East
♠ —                                     ♠ —
♥ 8                                     ♥ K Q
♦ —                                     ♦ —
♣ 10 9                                  ♣ K

                       You
                       South
                       ♠ 4
                       ♥ 4
                       ♦ ---
                       ♣ Q
```

You now lead your last trump. West's discard is immaterial, and you discard dummy's ♣8. East, however, has the problem. He has the unenviable choice of discarding the ♣K, setting up your ♣Q as a winner, or the ♥Q, permitting you to drop the king under dummy's ace and making the ♥J a winner.

♦ ♦ ♦ ♦

Squeeze possibilities are available in mundane contracts as well as in slams. The basic premises are the same. You have to reach a point where you can win all the remaining tricks except one. In the following example you are in a 4♥ contract.

*Dummy*
North
♠ Q 4 3
♥ Q 10 8 6
♦ 8 4 3
♣ A K 7

West
♠ A K 8 6
♥ 7
♦ J 9 5
♣ Q J 8 4 3

East
♠ J 10 7 5 2
♥ 5 3
♦ A Q 7 2
♣ 6 5

*You*
South
♠ 9
♥ A K J 9 4 2
♦ K 10 6
♣ 10 9 2

Contract: 4 ♥
Opening Lead: ♠A

When East plays a discouraging deuce on the opening ♠A lead, West switches to a small diamond. East wins the ace and returns the suit which you win with your king. You draw the outstanding trumps and exit with a diamond, which East's queen wins. The defenders now have their book.

You ruff the spade return and can win all except one of the remaining tricks. The squeeze can now come into play to garner that essential trick. You play all your trumps but one to reach this position:

```
                    Dummy
                    North
                    ♠ Q
                    ♥ —
                    ♦ —
                    ♣ A K 7
West                                        East
♠ K                                         ♠ J 10
♥ —                                         ♥ —
♦ —                                         ♦ —
♣ Q J 8                                     ♣ 6 5
                    You
                    South
                    ♠ —
                    ♥ 9
                    ♦ —
                    ♣ 10 9 2
```

You lead your last trump which squeezes West. If he discards the ♠K, it sets up dummy's ♠Q, and you discard the ♣7. If West discards the ♣8, dummy's ♠Q is discarded and the third club is set up for your winning trick.

Running a long suit is a good idea, if you can safely do it, even if there is not a true squeeze possibility. Defenders do make mistakes and discard the wrong cards under pressure. Defenders often believe they're being squeezed when actually they are not. A pseudo-squeeze is the fancy name for it.

♦ ♦ ♦ ♦

Here is an actual hand that occurred at a National Tournament in Orlando. I call it, "The Perils & Pearls of a Senior Player."

Sitting South our senior player "held" this hand:

♠ A Q
♥ A K Q 9 5 4
♦ K J 5
♣ A 5

With the opponents passing throughout, the bidding proceeded as follows:

| South | North |
|-------|-------|
| 2 ♣ | 3 ♦ |
| 3 ♥ | 4 ♥ |
| 4 NT | 5 ♦ |
| 5 NT | 6 ♣ |
| 7 NT | All Pass |

They were not playing waiting bids, so South fully expected to win six heart tricks, five diamonds plus the aces of spades and clubs. That added up to 13 tricks. The 7 NT contract looked like a good bet.

The opening lead was the ♥7 and Dummy came down:

♠ 9 8 3
♥ J 3 2
♦ A Q 8 7 2
♣ Q 2

Then, *"OOPS!"* The *Perils* of a senior moment set in. When fingering his cards again he discovered that what he thought was the ♥4 was really the ♦4. There were only five heart tricks not six. Now the 13 sure tricks were only 12 tricks.

This is the actual North-South Hand:

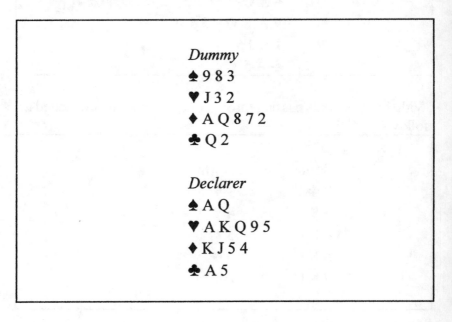

Dummy
♠ 9 8 3
♥ J 3 2
♦ A Q 8 7 2
♣ Q 2

Declarer
♠ A Q
♥ A K Q 9 5
♦ K J 5 4
♣ A 5

Where does our senior player go from here? Maybe the *Pearls* of years of experience will come to the rescue

West had led a passive ♥7. Assuming the hearts and diamond suits behave, one possible chance for the 13th trick is a successful spade finesse. But why did West lead one of *our* suits? Maybe he was afraid to lead away from his kings.

Let's try a squeeze play. It's more gratifying to say you won a grand slam by a squeeze than by just an ordinary lucky finesse.

The heart suit is run, discarding two spades from dummy. Now comes a key play. The ♣A is cashed, setting up dummy's ♣Q as a threat card. Four diamonds are played ending up in dummy.

This is the situation at this time:

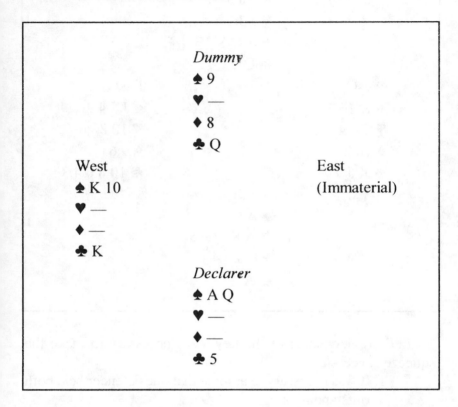

Dummy
♠ 9
♥ —
♦ 8
♣ Q

West
♠ K 10
♥ —
♦ —
♣ K

East
(Immaterial)

Declarer
♠ A Q
♥ —
♦ —
♣ 5

Dummy's ♦8 is played and declarer discards the ♣5. West has no winning option. He cannot discard the ♣K , that sets up dummy's ♣Q. He must discard the ♠10. Therefore a spade to South's ace drops West's ♠K. The squeeze wins the grand slam.

The complete hand:

```
                         North
                         ♠ 9 8 3
                         ♥ J 3 2
                         ♦ A Q 8 7 3
                         ♣ Q 2
     West                                    East
     ♠ K 10 7 6                              ♠ J 5 4 2
     ♥ 7 6 4                                 ♥ 10 8
     ♦ 10 2                                  ♦ 9 6
     ♣ K J 9 7                               ♣ 10 8 6 4 3
                         South
                         ♠ A Q
                         ♥ A K Q 9 5
                         ♦ K J 5 4
                         ♣ A 5
```

Let's review some of the key steps necessary to make the squeeze successful.

1. It was necessary to assume that one defender held both outstanding kings.
2. The hearts had to be run before the diamonds. The two discards from dummy had to be small spades.
3. Before running the diamonds, the ♣A had to be played to set up dummy's queen as a threat card.
4. The diamonds had to be played so that dummy is in the lead for the fifth diamond play

♦ ♦ ♦ ♦ ♦

*Deceptive Play*

Compared to games like poker, bridge is an "honest game." Whereas in poker you can act like you have a big hand, when in fact you have a bust, in bridge any deception must take a different form. You may deceive the opponents by *which card* you play, not by *how* you play it.

For example, you may not pause as if you are considering which card to play and then play the card, when actually you hold only a singleton. Declarer leads a queen and you pause as if to consider whether to cover it with the king, when in fact you do not have that card. That is a "no-no" in bridge.

Deceiving the opponents by which card you play, sometimes called falsecarding, is permitted and is often the wise thing to do.

Let's take this simple example from a notrump contract:

|  |  |
|---|---|
| | *Dummy* |
| | ♦ 9 4 |
| *You* | |
| ♦ A 10 6 5 | |

Your opening lead: ♦5

Dummy plays the ♦4, partner plays ♦J and declarer wins with the ♦K. Declarer plays another suit and you are in the lead again. This is the last outside entry to your hand. You would like to be able to run the diamond suit if at all possible. Partner could very well have correctly played the jack from a queen-jack holding. You therefore lead a small diamond to partner's hoped for queen so he could return the suit to your ace-ten.

But this was the actual setup:

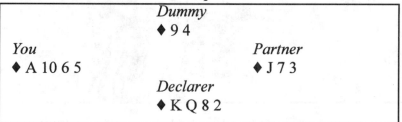

```
                    Dummy
                    ♦ 9 4
You                              Partner
♦ A 10 6 5                       ♦ J 7 3
                    Declarer
                    ♦ K Q 8 2
```

Declarer had falsecarded. He won the first trick with the king instead of the queen. If he had won the first trick with the queen you could not have gone wrong. You would have known partner could not have the king, because he would have played it on the opening lead. In that setup you would have tried to reach partner in another suit so that he could then lead the diamonds through the declarer.

Declarer's falsecard of the ♦K gave you a losing option. So remember when you are declarer it is wise for you to give the defense the losing option.

Falsecarding with honors is quite common, but it is the subtler forms using small cards that put you into the big leagues of deceptive play. A key aspect of deception is the necessity of playing cards at a normal pace with no undo hesitations.

This is one reason why I continually emphasize the need for planning before the first card is played from dummy. Don't let anyone, not even dummy, play a card from dummy even if it is a singleton. If you, as declarer, are planning a deceptive play on the opening lead, you must make your decision before it is your turn to play. To hesitate when you are about to play is a dead giveaway

Let's look at this hand:

```
                    Dummy
                    ♠ K J 8 4
                    ♥ 9 4 3
                    ♦ Q 7 5
                    ♣ 8 6 3
West                            East
♠ 9 5                           ♠ 7 3
♥ K Q 7                         ♥ 10 8 6
♦ 9 8 4 2                       ♦ A J 10 6
♣ A 10 9 4                      ♣ J 7 5 2
                    South
                    You
                    ♠ A Q 10 6 2
                    ♥ A J 5 2
                    ♦ K 3
                    ♣ K Q
```

Contract: 4 ♠ by South

Opening lead: ♥ K

You arrive at a 4 ♠ contract via a simple 1 ♠, 2 ♠, 4 ♠ auction. When the ♥K is tabled you count one club loser, one diamond loser and two possible heart losers. That's one more trick than you can afford to lose.

The only hope of avoiding a heart loser is subterfuge. You've planned your play. Play dummy's ♥3 and when East plays the ♥6 you follow smoothly with the ♥5 (not the ♥2).

The illusion you've attempted to create for West is that his partner has the ♥A 6 2 and is giving a high signal to continue the suit. When West takes the bait and continues hearts into your ♥A J you've eliminated one heart loser. The fancy name for this maneuver is "The Bath Coup."

The key to your success was that you did your planning before playing the first card from dummy. When it came your turn to play from your hand you were able to play your ♥5 without hesitation.

159

A few subtle deceptive tactics are available that can work in your favor. There are times when you want the defense to cover the card you play, usually an honor, and times when you would prefer that they do not cover immediately.

When you have a sequence, such as K Q J or Q J 10, lead the top card when you want it covered, a lower card if you prefer they hold off. With such sayings as "aces are meant to take kings" and "cover an honor with an honor," players are reluctant not to win the ace when they are offered the king. And if they do hold off, they may reveal its location by some hesitation.

Conversely, leading a lower card tends to have the defender refrain from covering. He may expect partner to be able to win the trick with an honor lower than his.

| Examples: | |
|---|---|
| Hand 1. | Hand 2. |
| *Dummy* | *Dummy* |
| North | North |
| A 7 6 | A 7 6 |
| West | West |
| K 5 4 | K 5 4 |
| *You* | *You* |
| South | South |
| Q J 10 | Q J 10 |

Hand 1. You would like to retain the ace in dummy even if the finesse is successful. You may need the ace as an entry for another suit or for some other valid reason. Lead the 10. West is less likely to cover with the king if he has it.

Hand 2. You would like your lead covered and then be able to get back into your hand. Play the queen. West is less likely to duck holding the king. .

The examples discussed here are just the tip of the iceberg. Deceptive play can be used by declarers or defenders. The opportunities are limitless. Just put your imagination to work.

## DUMMY REVERSAL

We are generally familiar with gaining extra tricks in suit contracts by ruffing cards in the hand with the fewer trumps (usually dummy), or by a cross-ruff between both hands.

Occasionally extra tricks can be made by ruffing in the hand with more trumps (usually the declarer) and drawing the trumps with the short hand (usually the dummy). This aptly is called, "A Dummy Reversal."

Here is an example:

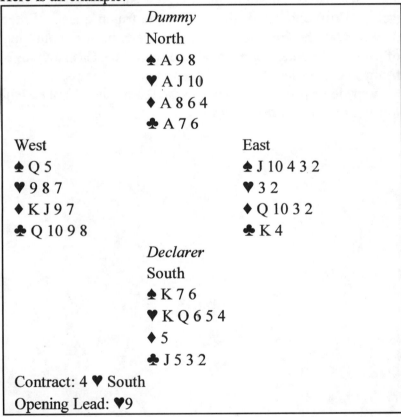

*Dummy*
North
♠ A 9 8
♥ A J 10
♦ A 8 6 4
♣ A 7 6

West
♠ Q 5
♥ 9 8 7
♦ K J 9 7
♣ Q 10 9 8

East
♠ J 10 4 3 2
♥ 3 2
♦ Q 10 3 2
♣ K 4

*Declarer*
South
♠ K 7 6
♥ K Q 6 5 4
♦ 5
♣ J 5 3 2

Contract: 4 ♥ South
Opening Lead: ♥9

The opponents have gotten off to a good safe trump lead. You can count nine tricks off the top. You could try to ruff a club in dummy. But that won't work because the defense will continue to play trumps each time they obtain the lead, exhausting dummy's trumps before you could ruff a club there.

What can you do? Try the dummy-reversal!

By ruffing three diamonds in your hand and then using dummy's three trumps to draw the trumps you wind up with six trump tricks instead of just five.

To execute the dummy reversal you have to handle your entries very carefully.

After winning the opening trump lead in dummy, play the ♦A and ruff a diamond in your hand. Play a small trump to dummy's jack and ruff another diamond with the trump queen. Enter dummy with the ♣A , and ruff the last diamond with your king of trumps. Re-enter dummy with the spade ace. Cash dummy's trump ace, drawing the last of the opponents trumps.

A spade to your king gives you the tenth trick. *The Dummy Reversal delivered the contract.*

♦ ♦ ♦ ♦ ♦

# OPENING LEADS
# IN SUIT CONTRACTS

♦ ♦ ♦ ♦

*Which Card and*
*Which Suit to Lead.*

♦ ♦ ♦ ♦

*Strategies of opening leads:*

♦ ♦ ♦ ♦

*Setting up High Cards.*
*When to Lead Trumps.*
*When to Lead a Singleton.*
*Forcing Declarer to Ruff.*

In the previous chapters the concentration has been on declarer play. Now, you are sitting at the other side of the table. You are one of the defenders.

The bidding's been concluded and the player on your right has become the declarer in a suit contract. That makes *you* the opening leader.

Being the opening leader is a mixed blessing. It gives you the opportunity to make the first strike. If you hit the declarer's Achilles' heel, it can be a devastating blow. On the other hand, you are making the initial play seeing only your own thirteen cards. Making the correct choice is not always simple.

What is the key difference between declarer and defenders' play? Before declarer has to play, he sees 100 percent of his assets ... all 26 cards ... *plus* your opening lead.

You see only your hand and do not see your partner's cards. Likewise, your partner has the same problem.

You therefore have a double job to accomplish with your opening lead. You have to make the most effective play and communicate with your partner at the same time.

Assume that the opponents are in a heart contract and you decide to make a lead from this diamond holding: ♦ Q J 10.

As far as you are concerned it makes no difference which card you play, they are all equal. But you have a partner. He may need some help.

Suppose you were to lead the 10; dummy's diamond holding is revealed and partner has to decide what to play:

|  | *Dummy* |  |
|---|---|---|
|  | ♦ K 8 6 |  |
| *Your Lead* |  | *Partner* |
| ♦ 10 |  | ♦ A 7 5 4 |

Declarer plays dummy's 6. What does your partner do? He might very well play the ace, giving the opponents a trick with the king, which they are not entitled to in this situation.

What would have happened if you had led the queen?

| | Dummy | |
|---|---|---|
| | ♦ K 8 6 | |
| *Your Lead* | | *Partner* |
| ♦ Q | | ♦ A 7 5 4 |

Partner would have no problem. If dummy played small, partner would play small. (You could then continue with the jack, etc.) If dummy rose with the king, partner would win with the ace and return the suit.

From this theory, the idea of leading the *top* of a sequence of equal cards evolved.

An agreement on a method of card leads is necessary for the defenders to be able to communicate with each other.

A system of standard leads is shown on the accompanying chart. Although there are other methods being used in some circles, the ones recommended here are most widely played. You can sit down at almost any table in any area and comfortably play these leads with little or no prior discussion.

First we will briefly go over some of the systemic reasons behind the various leads

1. When partner has not bid, a top of the sequence lead has a high priority. It combines an attacking value with a safety quality.

   K Q J, Q J 10 or J 10 9 8 leads may give up a trick or tricks to the declarer, but they are setting up your lower ranking honors as possible winners at the same time. If partner happens to hold the outstanding honors, so much the better.

2. When holding adjacent honors lead the top: A K X, lead the ace; K Q X, lead the king; Q J X, lead the queen; J 10 X, lead the jack.

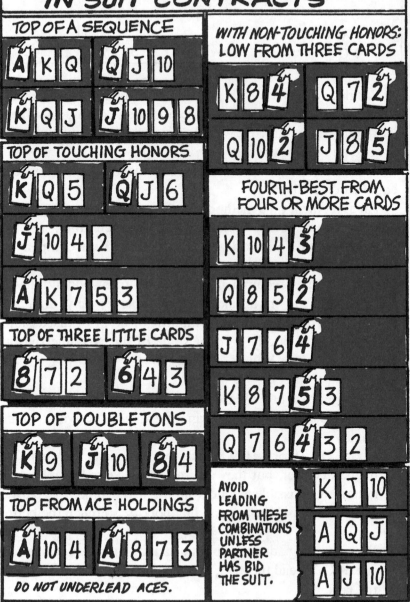

166

3. When leading from any two-card holding, you play high and then low: from K 2, you would lead king and then 2; from 8 7, lead 8 and then 7; from J 9, lead the jack and then 9.

   Exception: When holding A K, play the *king* followed by the *ace*. This will alert partner that it is a doubleton. (This will differentiate from A K X, where the standard procedure is to lead the ace followed by the king.)

4. When you wish to lead a suit containing three or more cards headed by an unsupported honor, lead a small card using the following method as a guide. Holding three cards headed by an honor, lead the lowest card. Holding four or more cards, lead "fourth-best." That is: Fourth card down from the top.

   A:  Holding Q 8 4, lead the 4
   B.  Holding K 6 2, lead the 2.
   C.  Holding Q 10 3, lead the 3.
   D.  Holding J 6 4, lead the 4.
   E.  Holding K 9 3 2, lead the 2.
   F.  Holding Q 8 6 5 3, lead the 5.

5. Leading from three small cards: The expert opinion of leads in this area varies greatly. All procedures have their pluses and minuses. The methods we are advocating are considered "standard." Lead the highest card. On your second opportunity play the next highest card.

   From: 8 6 2, lead the 8. On your next chance, play the 6. An alert partner will notice that the deuce has not been played and can assume that you hold that card. (From an original 8 2 holding, you would have played 8 2 and partner would have known you held a doubleton.)

   It is true that a knowledgeable declarer holding the deuce could have "false-carded" by not playing it, enticing you to reach an improper conclusion. This is one of the minuses we spoke about. But if your opponents are that sophisticated, you've got problems anyway, regardless of your methods. Other methods also have their problems.

6. Do not underlead the ace in suit contracts. If the suit you wish to lead contains the ace, lead the ace. Occasionally an underlead deceives the declarer, but more often it fools your partner. Many a declarer has won a trick with a singleton king as a result of an underlead of an ace.

To summarize this system for opening leads in suit contracts:
A. Lead top of a sequence.
B. Lead ace from A K X.
C. Lead high-low from two-card holdings.
D. Lead the top of adjacent honors.
E. Lead small from an unsupported honor; the lowest from a three-card holding and the "fourth-best" from four-or-more-card suits.
F. Lead top card from three small.
G. Do not underlead the ace in suit contracts.

Playing against a suit contract what card would you lead from these holdings?

| | | | | | |
|---|---|---|---|---|---|
| A. | K Q J 4 | E. | A K 8 5 | I. | Q 8 5 4 2 |
| B. | K 10 7 2 | F. | 7 2 | J. | A 10 9 7 |
| C. | Q 9 2 | G. | J 10 9 2 | K. | K Q 6 |
| D. | A 6 5 4 | H. | 8 6 3 | L. | Q J 9 |

A. Lead K: (Top of a sequence)
B. Lead 2: Fourth-best.
C. Lead 2: Low from an honor.
D. Lead A: Do not underlead ace in suit contracts.
E. Lead A: Lead A from A K X.
F. Lead 7: Lead high-low with doubleton.
G. Lead J: Top of a sequence.
H. Lead 8: Top of three little cards.
I. Lead 4: Fourth-best.
J. Lead A: Do not underlead ace in suit contracts.
K. Lead K: Lead K from K Q.
L. Lead Q: Top of two adjacent honors.

## STRATEGIES IN OPENING LEADS

Our concentration has been on the mechanics of opening leads in suit contracts to promote a clearer understanding between the partners of the defense.

We've been discussing *which* card to lead. Now we'll focus on *which* suit to lead and why.

The bidding and lack of bidding play a large part in determining the strategy of the defense. If your partner has bid a suit and you are on lead, it is usually a sound idea to lead his suit. In the course of a few rounds of bidding a great deal of information is often revealed which can help you plan your defensive strategy.

## I. ESTABLISHING HIGH CARDS AS WINNERS

In trump contracts it is frequently important to try to set up high card winners before declarer can obtain discards and ruff your winners.

Leading the top of a sequence from K Q J can prove very effective. It can establish Q J as quick defensive tricks.

A lead from Q J 10 is also desirable. Sometimes dummy has the king and your partner has the ace, in which case you've hit a bonanza. Occasionally your partner has one of the missing honors, the ace or king, which helps in the quick establishment of your lower honors. In any event, it is a safe lead giving up very little.

## Example 1

| Bidding: | West | North | East | South |
|---|---|---|---|---|
| *You* | — | Pass | Pass | 1♠ |
| West | Pass | 3♠ | Pass | 4♠ |

♠ 9 3                All Pass
♥ J 10 9 8
♦ 8 7 4
♣ Q J 10 7      Your opening lead?

You are on lead in South's 4♠ contract. You have two suits containing sequences. Which do you choose to lead?

Particularly in trump contracts, you should select the suit which has the probability of establishing lower ranking honors most quickly. In the club suit partner needs only one outstanding honor to set up your high cards as winners. In hearts, even if you could eventually establish winners, declarer's side may be void of the suit by that time and be able to ruff them.

The complete hand

```
                    North
                    ♠ K J 4 2
                    ♥ K 6 5 3
                    ♦ J 10
                    ♣ K 8 2
    West                            East
    ♠ 9 3                           ♠ 10 8
    ♥ J 10 9 8                      ♥ A 4 2
    ♦ 8 7 4                         ♦ K 6 5 3 2
    ♣ Q J 10 7                      ♣ A 9 4
                    South
                    ♠ A Q 7 6 5
                    ♥ Q 7
                    ♦ A Q 9
                    ♣ 6 5 3
```

The lead of the ♣Q hits pay dirt. Dummy has the king and your partner the ace. You rattle off three winners. Eventually, declarer must lose a trick to the ♦A for down one.

The ♥J opening lead would have permitted declarer to make his contract. Dummy would duck the lead and East would properly duck, as well. South's queen would win the trick. Declarer would draw trumps in two rounds winding up in dummy.

The diamond finesse would then be taken. It turns out to be successful and declarer discards a club loser from dummy on the third diamond. Declarer loses just two clubs and one heart and fulfills his 4♠ contract.

Example 2

| Bidding: | West | North | East | South |
|----------|------|-------|------|-------|
|          | —    | —     | Pass | Pass  |
|          | 1♥   | Pass  | 2♥   | Pass  |
|          | 4♥   | All Pass |    |       |

*You*
North
♠ A 6
♥ 9 6 5
♦ K Q J 8
♣ A 6 4 3

Your opening lead?

The lead of the ♦K appears the logical move. It could possibly set up the Q J as winners. Afterwards, the ♣A and ♠A may well provide the setting tricks.

Another alternative is to lead the ♠A and then the 6, hoping that partner has the king and you can obtain a ruff. But is this a realistic possibility?

An analysis of the bidding will show that partner is unlikely to hold any significant strength.

West opened the bidding and when his partner made a minimum response, he jumped to game. For West to leap to game after such a response he needs a 19 to 20 point hand.

**The opponents combined have approximately 25 to 26 points between them. Added to the 14 points you hold, that leaves** *no room* **for your partner to have a king.**

Careful attention to the bidding can be very helpful in determining the opening lead.

The complete hand

|  | North | |
|---|---|---|
|  | ♠ A 6 | |
|  | ♥ 9 6 5 | |
|  | ♦ K Q J 8 | |
|  | ♣ A 6 4 3 | |

| West | | East |
|---|---|---|
| ♠ K Q | | ♠ J 7 5 |
| ♥ A K J 7 2 | | ♥ Q 10 8 4 3 |
| ♦ 9 5 3 | | ♦ A 6 2 |
| ♣ K Q 7 | | ♣ J 2 |

|  | South | |
|---|---|---|
|  | ♠ 10 9 8 4 3 2 | |
|  | ♥ ------ | |
|  | ♦ 10 7 4 | |
|  | ♣ 10 9 8 5 | |

| Bidding: | West | North | East | South |
|---|---|---|---|---|
|  | — | — | Pass | Pass |
|  | 1♥ | Pass | 2♥ | Pass |
|  | 4♥ | All Pass | | |

Opening Lead: ♦K

172

The diamond lead defeats the contract.

Dummy's ace wins the opening lead. Trumps are drawn in three rounds. A club is surrendered to North's ace. North cashes the ♦K Q and the ♠A winding up with four tricks.

If the opening lead had been the ♠A (or even the ♣A) the contract could not be defeated. Declarer would win the spade continuation (or win the ♦A, if North switches to the ♦K), draw the outstanding trumps and play dummy's high spade discarding a diamond loser from his hand. Declarer winds up losing only one diamond, one club and one spade.

Likewise, if the ♣A was the opening lead, declarer could discard a losing diamond from dummy on his third high club.

Leads of aces tend to establish *declarer's* secondary honors. The lead of the top of a sequence sets up *your* secondary honors.

## II. *RUFFING DECLARER'S HIGH CARDS*

In suit contracts winning tricks by ruffing is a delightful prospect.

If partner has bid a suit and you have a singleton or a doubleton, it is usually an excellent lead. It can accomplish two things at once: Permit partner to make tricks in the suit and let you ruff any losers he might have.

Example:

You lead your singleton in partner's spade suit and dummy's hand is tabled.

North

♠ 9 5 4

♥ A 7 5 2

♦ 10 9 8

♣ K Q 5

Partner wins your lead with the ♠K. He cashes the ♠A, on which you discard a diamond, and continues with the ♠J. South covers it with the ♠Q which you ruff.

Eventually partner wins a minor suit ace, defeating the contract.

This is the complete hand:

```
                    North
                    ♠ 9 5 4
                    ♥ A 7 5 2
                    ♦ 10 9 8
                    ♣ K Q 5
    West                          East
    ♠ 8                           ♠ A K J 10 7 2
    ♥ 10 8 4                      ♥ 6
    ♦ 7 6 4 3                     ♦ A 2
    ♣ J 10 9 7 3                  ♣ 8 6 4 2
                    South
                    ♠ Q 6 3
                    ♥ K Q J 9 3
                    ♦ K Q J 5
                    ♣ A
```

Leading a singleton in partner's suit is certainly a good idea.

But when do you lead a singleton when it is *not likely* to be in your partner's suit?

## SOME GUIDELINES ON SINGLETON LEADS

When you are leading a singleton in a suit which may be the opponents' suit, care must be taken.

Yes, do lead a singleton when these conditions exist:

1. You have first or second round control of the trump suit, and...
2. A way of reaching partner in another suit.

## Example

The bidding has gone:

| West | North | East | South |
|------|-------|------|-------|
| --- | --- | --- | 1♣ |
| 1♦ | 1♠ | Pass | 2♠ |
| Pass | 4♠ | All Pass | |

*You*
East
- ♠ A 6 3
- ♥ 8 7 6 5 4 2
- ♦ J 6 3
- ♣ 4

You are on lead against North's 4♠ contract, what do you lead?

1. You have a singleton in clubs which the opponents have bid.

2. You have the ace of trump.

3. You have a way of reaching partner in diamonds, his bid suit.

Why do you need trump control?
If you don't have control, the declarer can draw the trumps and you would have none with which to ruff.

**With trump control, you can stop declarer from drawing them, reach partner in his diamond suit and he can play a club for you to ruff.**

| | | | |
|---|---|---|---|
| | **North** | | |
| | ♠ K J 9 8 2 | | |
| | ♥ A 3 | | |
| | ♦ Q 9 8 | | |
| | ♣ Q 9 6 | | |

| **West** | | **East** | |
|---|---|---|---|
| ♠ 5 | | ♠ A 6 3 | |
| ♥ Q 10 9 | | ♥ 8 7 6 5 4 2 | |
| ♦ A K 10 4 2 | | ♦ J 6 3 | |
| ♣ J 10 7 5 | | ♣ 4 | |

| | |
|---|---|
| | **South** |
| | ♠ Q 10 7 4 |
| | ♥ K J |
| | ♦ 7 5 |
| | ♣ A K 8 3 2 |

Bidding:

| West | North | East | South |
|---|---|---|---|
| — | — | --- | 1♣ |
| 1♦ | 1♠ | Pass | 2♠ |
| Pass | 4♠ | All Pass | |

Opening Lead: ♣4

This is one hand where *not* leading partner's suit is correct, because you have a *valid* reason. You want to retain that option to reach partner later so that he can play a club for you to ruff.

The scenario would go something like this:

After declarer wins the opening club lead with his queen, he leads a trump and you hop up with your ace. You now play the ♦3 to partner's king. He may very well say to himself, "Gee, partner had a diamond after all. Why did he make an opening lead of a club? It must have been a singleton!"

He plays a club which you ruff. You return another diamond to his ace. He in turn leads another club for you to trump. You've set the contract two tricks. You've won the ace of trump, two diamonds and two ruffs.

The complete pre-conditions existed for the singleton lead: You had a singleton, first round control of trump and a way of reaching partner.

NO! Do not lead a singleton:
1. When it would establish the opponents' suit. Without the safeguards indicated previously, you are doing declarer's work for him.
2. When you would be ruffing with what would have been trump winners anyway. If your trump holding is something like Q J 10, K Q, A K, or K 2, you would be ruffing with natural trump tricks. You may be better off trying to establish some tricks in another side suit and win your trump tricks naturally.

### WHEN TO GIVE PARTNER A RUFF

Careful attention to the bidding can give you a clue that partner may have a singleton.

| Example | South |
|---------|-------|
| | ♠ J 10 3 |
| | ♥ A 2 |
| | ♦ A 6 4 2 |
| | ♣ 10 7 3 2 |

| Bidding: | West | North | East | South |
|----------|------|-------|------|-------|
| | — | Pass | 1♥ | Pass |
| | 2♣ | Pass | 3♣ | Pass |
| | 3♥ | Pass | 4♥ | All Pass |
| Opening Lead: ? | | | | |

You hold the South hand, hear the above bidding and have to decide what to lead. What have you learned?

178

1. East's opening bid: Five hearts or more.
2. West's response: Possibly, four clubs or more.
3. East's rebid: Most likely four clubs.
4. West's rebid: Three hearts.
5. East: Places the contract at 4♥; most likely has five hearts and four clubs.

With no guidelines from the bidding, the ♠J would seem a likely choice as an opening lead. But what do you suspect about the East-West club holding? They may have at least eight clubs between them. You have four clubs. That leaves your partner with room for only one club.

A club lead now assumes a high priority. You are in fact leading *partner's* singleton. An additional consideration is that you have first-round control of the trump suit.

The opening lead: ♣2.

The complete hand

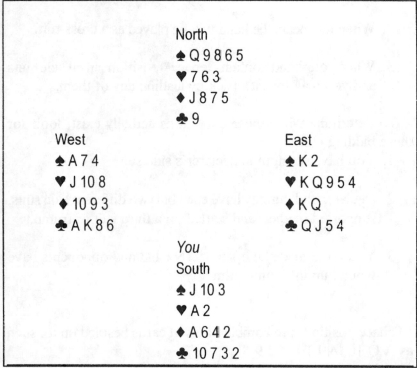

North
♠ Q 9 8 6 5
♥ 7 6 3
♦ J 8 7 5
♣ 9

West
♠ A 7 4
♥ J 10 8
♦ 10 9 3
♣ A K 8 6

East
♠ K 2
♥ K Q 9 5 4
♦ K Q
♣ Q J 5 4

*You*
South
♠ J 10 3
♥ A 2
♦ A 6 4 2
♣ 10 7 3 2

179

After declarer wins the club lead, you win the trump return with your ace.  Lead the ♣3 which partner ruffs.

He leads a diamond to your ace and you play another club for partner to ruff.  Two aces and two ruffs set the contract.


## III.  *WHEN TO LEAD TRUMP*

This area of defense again emphasizes the importance of paying close attention to the bidding.  It is the most valuable tool of the opening leader.  It becomes the seeing-eye for your blind leads.

Lead trump:
1. When it appears dummy's trumps will be needed to ruff losers.

2. When it appears the hand will be played as a cross-ruff.

3. When your hand contains tenace* positions in all side suits and you may forfeit a trick by leading any of them.

To determine when these conditions actually exist, look for these bidding clues.
1. You have strength in declarer's side suit.

2. Declarer and dummy have each bid two different side suits, supported neither, and settled on a third suit as trump.

3. You have made an opening 1NT bid and opponents have wound up in a suit contract.


*Tenace positions are combinations of cards best led up to, such as A Q 10, A J 10, K J 9.

Example 1.

| Bidding: | West | North | East | South |
|---|---|---|---|---|
| | Pass | Pass | Pass | 1♠ |
| | Pass | 1NT | Pass | 2♥ |
| | Pass | 3♥ | Pass | 4♥ |

You, West, hold:

♠ K J 9 8

♥ A 6 5

♦ J 10 9 7

♣ 6 5

Your lead?

What have you learned from the bidding?

A.   South's opening bid: Five or more spades, 13+ pts.

B.   North's response: Two or less spades, 6 to 10 pts.

C.   South's rebid: Four or more hearts, at least five spades.

D.   North's rebid: His hand has evidently improved with the magic fit. Has at least four hearts, 8 to 10 pts.

E.   South's final bid: 16+ pts. On a revalued basis.

These are the areas you are fairly sure of: You know at least nine of South's cards, four hearts and five spades. That leaves shortness in the other two suits.

North's hand is obviously short in spades. Declarer's partnership is on the borderline in high-card points. Their hopes for game depend greatly on their distribution and ruffing values.

You have three possible spade tricks, if they are not trumped in dummy. To cut down dummy's ruffing power, the logic dictates: Lead a trump.

In this case, a small trump lead is indicated. You desire to draw three rounds of trump if you can. If partner should obtain the lead before you do, he may still have a trump to lead to your ace. At that time you have the opportunity to play your third trump.

The complete hand:

**North**
- ♠ 4 2
- ♥ Q 10 8 4
- ♦ K 8 5
- ♣ K J 8 4

**West**
- ♠ K J 9 8
- ♥ A 6 5
- ♦ J 10 9 7
- ♣ 6 5

**East**
- ♠ 5 3
- ♥ 3 2
- ♦ 6 4 2
- ♣ A Q 10 9 3 2

**South**
- ♠ A Q 10 7 6
- ♥ K J 9 7
- ♦ A Q 3
- ♣ 7

| Bidding: | West | North | East | South |
|---|---|---|---|---|
| | Pass | Pass | Pass | 1♠ |
| | Pass | 1NT | Pass | 2♥ |
| | Pass | 3♥ | Pass | 4♥ |
| | All Pass | | | |

Opening Lead: ♥5

Declarer wins the opening lead in his hand, plays a club, finessing the jack, which loses to East's queen. East continues the strategy of drawing trumps. You win with the ace and lead your last trump, which is won in dummy. A spade finesse is attempted which you win and exit with a diamond.

Declarer is held to three trump tricks, three diamonds, one spade and one ruff, for a two trick set. If trumps are never played by the defenders, declarer makes his contract.

Example 2.

| Bidding: | West | North | East | South |
|----------|------|-------|------|-------|
| | — | — | — | Pass |
| | 1♦ | Pass | 1♥ | Pass |
| | 1♠ | Pass | 2♦ | All Pass |

You, North, hold:

♠ K J 9 5
♥ J 5
♦ 7 6 2
♣ K J 10 7

The auction in this hand revealed that West, the opening bidder, did not support responder's suit, and East did not support West's second bid suit. East settled by giving a preference to West's opening bid.

The opening lead of a trump is indicated.

The complete hand:

North
♠ K J 9 5
♥ J 5
♦ 7 6 2
♣ K J 10 7

West
♠ A Q 10 3
♥ 9 2
♦ K J 8 5 3
♣ A 3

East
♠ 4 2
♥ A Q 7 6
♦ Q 9 4
♣ 9 5 4 2

South
♠ 8 7 6
♥ K 10 8 4 3
♦ A 10
♣ Q 8 6

Opening Lead: ♦7

The opening diamond is won by South's ace, the ♦10 is continued and won by dummy's queen. A spade is led to West's queen, North's king winning the trick. North continues the tactic of leading trumps. East, now exhausted of trumps, can no longer ruff a spade. Declarer is held to only seven tricks, for one down.

Example 3:.

| Bidding: | West | North | East | South |
|---|---|---|---|---|
| | — | — | 1 NT | Pass |
| | Pass | 2♥ | All Pass | |

You, East, hold: ♠ A Q J 10  ♥ 8 5  ♦ K J 7 5  ♣ A Q 10

What do you lead?

You've opened the bidding with 1NT, North overcalled 2♥, and you are now on lead.

Leading any of the side suits may very well give up a trick to the declarer. You, therefore, make a passive lead of a trump. The complete hand:

North
♠ K 6
♥ A K 10 9 6 3
♦ Q 4 2
♣ K 3

West
♠ 8 7 5
♥ J 4
♦ 10 9 8
♣ J 9 8 7 6

East
♠ A Q J 10
♥ 8 5
♦ K J 7 5
♣ A Q 10

South
♠ 9 4 3 2
♥ Q 7 2
♦ A 6 3
♣ 5 4 2

Opening Lead: ♥8

Any other opening lead automatically gives declarer his eighth trick. Careful defense is still necessary to defeat the contract, but the passive opening lead of a trump is the only hope for the defense to succeed.

## IV: *FORCE DECLARER TO RUFF*

An opening lead in your side's strong suit, and continued playing of that suit, forcing declarer to ruff, can be an effective defensive tactic. This is particularly true when one of the defenders holds four trumps.

Your hope is that after a couple of ruffs declarer will have fewer trumps than one of the defenders. Declarer may very well lose control of the hand.

As the opening leader, it is easier to recognize this tactic when *you* hold four trumps. Special attention to the bidding is often necessary to determine when *partner* has four trumps.

| Bidding: | West | North | East | South |
|----------|------|-------|------|-------|
|          | —    | —     | 1♠   | Pass  |
|          | 2♠   | 3♣    | 4♠   | All Pass |

You, South, hold:

♠ 5
♥ 9 8 5 4 3 2
♦ 10 3 2
♣ A 9 5

What is your opening lead?

Your partner had made a 3♣ overcall. It seems like a good idea to lead his suit. You make your opening lead: ♣A

Dummy comes down:

♠ K 9 3
♥ 10 6
♦ Q J 8 5
♣ 10 4 3 2

Your ♣A wins the trick as partner plays the 8 and declarer the 7. What do you do now?

Partner certainly started with a five-card club suit. Simple arithmetic tells you that declarer is out of clubs and will ruff the next club. Do you continue another club or do you switch to another suit?

Another bit of arithmetic indicates that your partner may have as many as four trumps, if declarer holds only a five-card trump suit. So you decide to play the forcing game and play another club which declarer ruffs.

The complete hand:

| | North | | |
|---|---|---|---|
| | ♠ 10 8 7 4 | | |
| | ♥ A K | | |
| | ♦ 7 6 | | |
| | ♣ K Q J 8 6 | | |
| **West** | | **East** | |
| ♠ K 9 3 | | ♠ A Q J 6 2 | |
| ♥ 10 6 | | ♥ Q J 7 | |
| ♦ Q J 8 5 | | ♦ A K 9 4 | |
| ♣ 10 4 3 2 | | ♣ 7 | |
| | **South** | | |
| | ♠ 5 | | |
| | ♥ 9 8 5 4 3 2 | | |
| | ♦ 10 3 2 | | |
| | ♣ A 9 5 | | |

Bidding:

| | West | North | East | South |
|---|---|---|---|---|
| | --- | --- | 1♠ | Pass |
| | 2♠ | 3♣ | 4♠ | All Pass |
| Opening Lead: ♣A | | | | |

The second club lead does indeed reduce declarer's holding to four trumps. No matter how he wriggles, declarer must be defeated as long as North continues to play clubs whenever he obtains the lead.

Declarer's safest procedure to prevent a disaster is to try to establish a heart trick first. He leads a heart to dummy's ten which North wins with the king. Another club forces declarer to ruff. North wins the next heart lead and plays a club which declarer ruffs.

At this time, North has *four* trumps while declarer has just *two* and dummy three. Declarer doesn't know this and hopes for a 3-2 trump break to make his contract. He plays the A Q of trump and learns the sad news. He must go down two tricks.

If the defense did not continually play clubs, declarer may well have made the contract easily.

Prove it to yourself. Try the defense without continuing clubs after the opening lead.

Statistically you're going to be an opening leader 25 % of the time. Learn to listen carefully to the bidding to help determine your strategy. After selecting the suit to lead, choose the correct card which conforms to your system.

This way you can make the most effective lead and communicate with your partner at the same time.

Your blind leads may not be so blind after all.

♦ ♦ ♦ ♦ ♦

# OPENING LEADS
# IN NOTRUMP
# CONTRACTS

### *Which Card*
### *and Which Suit*
### *to Lead*
♦ ♦ ♦
### *Strategy of*
### *Opening Leads*
♦ ♦ ♦
### *Rule of Eleven*

Just as notrump play differs from suit contract play, so does the opening lead.

In notrump, the defense usually tries to establish a suit by knocking out declarer's stoppers, regain the lead and run the suit.

Because the overall strategy is different than in suit contracts, the specific cards led are different as well. The card played has to be effective and carry a message to partner at the same time.

The accompanying chart spells out the mechanics of opening leads in notrump. It is divided in two parts:

1. Leading your own best suit.
2. Leading partner's bid or implied suit.

### LEADING YOUR OWN BEST SUIT

1. If the suit contains a sequence, leading the top of the sequence is usually a safe and effective lead.

Examples: _K_ Q J 6 5; _Q_ J 10 4 3; _Q_ J 10 4.

2. If the suit has an interior sequence, the top of the interior sequence is the recommended lead. It may give up a trick to the declarer, but it often quickly establishes the suit.

Examples: A _J_ 10 9 3; K _J_ 10 9 5; A _Q_ J 9 3.

3. Occasionally you have "broken sequences", such as: _K_ Q 10 9 5; _Q_ J 9 8 2. It is often wise to lead the top of a broken sequence.

4. If your best suit does not have sequence conditions as shown above, a "fourth-best" lead is indicated.

Examples: A 10 7 _6_; K 9 7 _4_ 2; Q 10 7 _4_; A K 7 _5_ 3; Q J 6 _5_.

Leading "fourth-best", or more accurately stated, fourth card down, permits your partner to use the rule of eleven to help him determine which card to play. A definition and discussion of this rule will follow later in this chapter.

# OPENING LEADS
## IN NOTRUMP CONTRACTS

| LEADING YOUR OWN BEST SUIT... | LEADING PARTNER'S BID (OR IMPLIED) SUIT... |
|---|---|

**TOP OF A SEQUENCE**

K Q J 8 3

Q J 10 7

J 10 9 6 5 2

**TOP OF A BROKEN SEQUENCE**

K Q 10 9

Q J 9 8 3

**TOP OF INTERIOR SEQUENCE**

A J 10 9 6

A Q J 10 4

**FOURTH-BEST FROM HONORS**

K 9 7 5 2

Q J 6 3

**WITH NON-TOUCHING HONORS: LOW FROM THREE CARDS**

K 8 4     A 7 2

Q 10 2     J 8 5

**FOURTH-BEST FROM FOUR OR MORE CARDS**

K 10 4 3 2

A 7 5 2

**TOP OF TOUCHING HONORS**

K Q 5     Q J 6 4

**TOP OF THREE LITTLE CARDS**

8 6 3     7 5 2

**TOP OF DOUBLETONS**

K 9     J 10     8 4

IN NOTRUMP YOU **DO** UNDERLEAD ACES.

You are on lead in a notrump contract. Your partner has *not* bid. What card do you lead from each of the following holdings?

| | | |
|---|---|---|
| 1. A J 9 4 2 | 6. K Q 6 2 | 11. J 10 9 7 |
| 2. K Q J 4 2 | 7. K J 10 9 4 | 12. A 5 4 2 |
| 3. Q 10 7 6 | 8. Q 7 6 5 | 13. Q J 6 2 |
| 4. Q J 10 5 | 9. A J 10 8 5 | 14. K 4 3 2 |
| 5. Q J 9 8 5 | 10. A K 9 5 2 | 15. A Q J 8 3 |

| | | |
|---|---|---|
| 1. | Lead 4: | Fourth-best. |
| 2. | Lead K: | Top of a sequence. |
| 3. | Lead 6: | Fourth-best. |
| 4. | Lead Q: | Top of a sequence. |
| 5. | Lead Q: | Top of broken sequence. |
| 6. | Lead 2: | Fourth-best. |
| 7. | Lead J: | Top of an interior sequence. |
| 8. | Lead 5: | Fourth-best. |
| 9. | Lead J: | Top of an interior sequence. |
| 10. | Lead 5: | Fourth-best. |
| 11. | Lead J: | Top of a sequence. |
| 12. | Lead 2: | Fourth-best. |
| 13. | Lead 2: | Fourth-best. |
| 14. | Lead 2: | Fourth-best. |
| 15. | Lead Q: | Top of an interior sequence. |

## *LEADING PARTNER'S BID OR IMPLIED SUIT*

Leading partner's bid or implied suit requires a different set of disciplines.

1. Lead low from a holding of three cards headed by one honor or by two non-contiguous honors.

Examples: A 7 *3*; K 8 *5*; Q 9 *2*; J 6 *3*; Q10 *2*; A10 *3*.

2. With four or more cards headed by one honor or two non-contiguous honors, lead fourth-best.

Examples: A 9 6 *4*; K 9 8 *7* 2; K J 4 *2* Q 10 6 *3*.

3. When holding two or more contiguous honors, it is usually wise to lead the top of the honors.

Examples: **K** Q 3; _**Q**_ J 5; _**J**_ 10 4; _**Q**_ J 7 3; _**Q**_ J 10.

4. With a holding containing no honors, lead the top of three cards, "fourth-best" from four or more cards.

Examples: _**9**_ 7 2; _**8**_ 4 3; _**8**_ 7 6; _**5**_ 4 2; 8 7 4 _**2**_.

5. From any two-card holding, lead the top card first.

Examples: **K** 2; _**Q**_ 5; _**10**_ 9; _**A**_ 5; _**3**_ 2; _**8**_ 6; _**Q**_ J.

## LEADING PARTNER'S SUIT

Again, you are on lead against a notrump contract, This time your partner has bid and you are leading *his* suit. Which card do you lead from each of the following holdings?

| | | | |
|---|---|---|---|
| 1. | 8 2 | 8. | Q J 5 3 |
| 2. | A 2 | 9. | 8 7 5 2 |
| 3. | A J 2 | 10. | J 10 9 |
| 4. | K 7 6 4 | 11. | K 5 |
| 5. | K Q 4 | 12. | K 10 3 2 |
| 6. | Q 5 2 | 13. | J 9 8 3 2 |
| 7. | 8 4 2 | 14. | A 6 3 2 |

1. Lead 8, top of a doubleton.
2. Lead A, top of a doubleton
3. Lead 2, low from three with non-touching honors.
4. Lead 4, fourth-best from an honor.
5. Lead K, top of touching honors.
6. Lead 2, low from three to an honor.
7. Lead 8, top of three little.
8. Lead Q, top of touching honors.
9. Lead 2, fourth-best from four little cards.
10. Lead J, top of a sequence.
11. Lead K, top of a doubleton.
12. Lead 2, fourth-best from non-touching honors.
13. Lead 3, fourth-best of five-card holding.
14. Lead 2, fourth-best from an honor.

Notice some of the differences between the leading procedures when your partner has bid a suit and when he has not.

When he's bid the suit: You are *expecting* him to have an honor. When he hasn't: You are *hoping* he has an honor.

For example: From identical holdings, Q J 7 2:
A.   If he's bid the suit, lead the queen.
B.   If he hasn't lead the deuce.

A.  Partner's bid the suit.
1.   Dummy may have the king and partner the ace. Bingo! You've hit pay dirt.

2.   Partner may have the king and declarer the ace. Partner will play an encouraging card asking you to continue the suit whenever you obtain the lead again.

3.   Partner may have the ace and declarer, the king. Partner has the option of overtaking the queen and continuing the suit, or playing an encouraging card allowing declarer to win the king. In either event the suit is established whenever you side regains the lead.

B.    When partner has not bid the suit you are *hoping* he has either the 10, king or ace. If he doesn't have any of those honors, you at least retain a stopper against the opponent winning more than three tricks in the suit.

Notice another important difference between notrump and suit contract opening leads. In notrump you generally *underlead* aces while in a suit contract you do not.

◆ ◆ ◆ ◆ ◆

In simple uncontested auctions the opponents arrive at 3NT contracts. What are your opening leads with these holdings?

---

Example 1.

♠ 8 7 5
♥ A J 9 5 2
♦ Q J 10
♣ 3 2

Opening Lead:

---

Example 2.

♠ A 4 3 2
♥ 9 8
♦ Q J 10 8 2
♣ 8 7

Opening Lead:

---

Example 3

♠ Q J 10 7
♥ 8 6 3
♦ Q J 10 7
♣ 6 2

Opening Lead:

---

1. Lead ♥5.  This lead has the best chance of establishing the suit, if partner has as little as the ♥10 and a way of later obtaining the lead. An opening lead of a ♦Q is safer but has much less chance of establishing enough tricks to defeat a 3NT contract.

2. Lead ♦Q.  This top of a sequence lead combines safety with a suit that has a good possibility of establishment. Partner needs only one honor for quick setting up of the suit. Failing that, partner may have an outside entry enabling him to lead the suit again. You have an outside entry to permit you to run the suit when established.

3. Lead ♠Q.  When you have a choice between suits, it is usually more effective to lead the major suit. Good players often try to wind up in a 4♥ or 4♠ contract in preference to 3NT. When no attempt is made to reach such a major suit contract, the notrump bidders are more likely to have their strength in the *minor* suits. Hence the major suit lead has a greater chance of success.

How effective are the leads in actual practice?

Here is the complete hand in Example 1.

```
Dealer: North
                              North
                              ♠ Q 10 2
                              ♥ K Q 4
                              ♦ A 6
                              ♣ K Q J 10 7

            West                              East
            ♠ J 6 4 3                         ♠ 8 7 5
            ♥ 10 8 3                          ♥ A J 9 5 2
            ♦ 5 4 3                           ♦ Q J 10
            ♣ A 5 4                           ♣ 3 2

                              South
                              ♠ A K 9
                              ♥ 7 6
                              ♦ K 9 8 7 2
                              ♣ 9 8 6
```

| Bidding: | West | North | East | South |
|----------|------|-------|------|-------|
|          | —    | 1 NT  | Pass | 3 NT  |
|          | All Pass |   |      |       |

Opening Lead: ♥5

On your opening lead West plays the 10 which North captures with the queen. Declarer needs to develop club tricks to make his contract. Your partner wins the club lead with the ace and returns the ♥8 through declarer's king. You run four heart tricks which, in addition to partner's club trick, defeats the contract. Once you hit on the proper lead, declarer could not make his contract.

An alternative line of play for the declarer was to hold up winning the initial heart lead. When partner continues the suit by playing the ♥8, you counteract declarer's strategy by refusing to win the trick.

197

When partner later obtains the lead with the ♣A, he still has another heart left to reach your hand. No matter how declarer wriggled he was doomed.

Making the first strike is so important. In 3NT contracts the declarer's hand usually has the preponderance of the high card strength. If given the slightest opportunity, declarer can quickly establish sufficient tricks to fulfill the contract.

Notice how the "safe" lead of the ♦Q would have permitted the declarer to make 3NT with ease.

North would have immediately set up the club suit and undoubtedly would have wound up with an overtrick.

♦ ♦ ♦ ♦ ♦

This is the complete hand from Example 2.

| Dealer: West | | |
|---|---|---|
| | **North** | |
| | ♠ K 9 8 | |
| | ♥ A 10 7 5 | |
| | ♦ 7 4 3 | |
| | ♣ 10 9 3 | |
| **West** | | **East** |
| ♠ Q J 7 | | ♠ 10 6 5 |
| ♥ Q 4 2 | | ♥ K J 6 3 |
| ♦ K 6 5 | | ♦ A 9 |
| ♣ Q 6 4 2 | | ♣ A K J 5 |
| | **South** | |
| | ♠ A 4 3 2 | |
| | ♥ 9 8 | |
| | ♦ Q J 10 8 2 | |
| | ♣ 8 7 | |
| Opening Lead: ♦Q | | |

The top of a sequence diamond lead sets the defense in motion.

198

Declarer wins the ♦A and attempts to establish the heart suit. Your partner takes the ♥Q with the ace, and returns a diamond. Declarer holds up one round, but you continue diamonds setting up the suit.

Declarer runs his clubs and tries to cash three heart tricks. However, the suit does not break and he has to give up the lead in spades. Your ace wins and you cash the balance of your diamonds.

You've won one heart, one spade and three diamond tricks, defeating the contract.

Establishing the diamond suit was the key to the defense. An opening lead of a spade, for example, and a spade continuation would have done declarer's work for him; A spade trick would be established for the declarer. All he would then have to do is give up a heart trick, giving him two hearts, one spade, two diamonds and four clubs for the successful fulfillment of his contract.

♦ ♦ ♦ ♦ ♦

In the following examples the bidding is a little more complex with your side entering the auction.

Example 1.

Bidding:

| West | North | East | South |
|------|-------|------|-------|
| --- | --- | 1♦ | 1♠ |
| 1NT | Pass | 2♣ | Pass |
| 2NT | All Pass | | |

*You*

North: ♠ Q 4 3  ♥ J 9 6 4 3  ♦ Q J 9  ♣ 6 5

Your opening lead?

In this hand your partner competed by bidding 1♠.

Your left hand opponent bid both diamonds and clubs.

Leading either of them would undoubtedly help declarer establish that suit.

Hearts is *your* best suit. But is it *your side's* best suit? Even if you were able to eventually establish the hearts, you have no outside high-card entries to enable you to run the suit.

Your partner's 1♠ overcall indicates five or more cards and should contain one of the top honors. With at least eight cards between you, your side's best suit is therefore spades. Leading your partner's suit is usually a good idea anyway.

Now that you've decided to lead spades, what card do you lead from Q 4 3?

**The chart tells us to lead: ♠3**

This is the complete hand.

```
Dealer: South
                        North
                        ♠ Q 4 3
                        ♥ J 9 6 4 3
                        ♦ Q J 9
                        ♣ 6 5

        West                            East
        ♠ K J 9                         ♠ 5 2
        ♥ A 10 7 5                      ♥ K 2
        ♦ 10 2                          ♦ A K 8 7 3
        ♣ Q 4 3 2                       ♣ K 10 8 7

                        South
                        ♠ A 10 8 7 6
                        ♥ Q 8
                        ♦ 6 5 4
                        ♣ A J 9

Contract: 2NT by West
Opening Lead: ♠3
```

Partner's ace wins your opening spade lead and a spade is continued. West finesses with the jack and your queen wins the trick. Your last spade is played. West wins as your partner's spade suit is established.

Declarer has a number of ways to go at this point, none of which succeeds with correct defense.

1.  If he attempts to establish diamonds, you win a trick there. Eventually partner has to obtain the lead with the ♣A and can run the balance of the spade suit to defeat the contract

2.  If declarer tries to establish clubs by finessing with the 10, South wins with the jack and immediately runs the spades and the ♣A, for a one trick set.

3.  If declarer makes a series of inspired plays, the defense will still prevail with the proper judgment. A diamond is led to dummy's king. The ♣7 is played, South covers with the ♣9 and declarer wins the ♣Q. The ace and another diamond are played which your ♦Q wins.

    At this point you have to decide between leading a heart or a club. You may realize that declarer would not have bid notrump twice without having the ♥A as a stopper. A switch to a club is indicated. This results in a two-trick set.

In analyzing the hand further some may say that the opponents' bidding was not the best. A club contract would have been far superior. That is true. However, you have to be able to take advantage of opponents' indiscretions.

Returning to the mechanics of the opening lead, this hand is a good illustration of the rationale behind leading *small* from a three-card holding headed by an honor.

The question has been asked many times, "Why don't you lead the *queen* from Q 4 3 when it's partner's suit?"

By isolating the spade suit from the previous hand the correct answer becomes clear.

```
                            Dummy
                            ♠ 5 2
Leader:       ♠ Q 4 3                      ♠ A 10 8 7 6
                            Declarer
                            ♠ K J 9
```

The correct lead of the ♠3 permits declarer to win only *one trick* in the suit, with the king.

The lead of the queen assures *two tricks* to the declarer, the king *and the jack*.

---

Example 2:

| Bidding: | West | North | East | South |
|----------|------|-------|------|-------|
|          | —    | —     | —    | 1♦    |
|          | Pass | 1♠    | Dbl  | 1 NT  |
|          | Pass | 2 NT  | Pass | 3 NT  |
|          | All Pass |   |      |       |

West

♠ Q J 10 9 3   ♥ 8 5 3   ♦ J 10 9   ♣ 6 5

Determine your opening lead.

---

What suit do you lead? What card do you lead? Why?

If the bidding had simply gone 1NT, 2NT, 3NT, the opening lead decision would be easy: the ♠Q. However, that was not the auction. Bidding often supplies clues that reveal distributions and strengths of the players that help in making a reasoned decision for an opening lead.

An analysis of the bidding reveals:
1. South's 1♦ bid:: At least three diamonds, 13+ points.
2. North's 1♠: Four or more spades, 6+points.
3. East's double: A take-out double indicating length and strength in the unbid suits, hearts and clubs.
4. South's 1 NT: Moderate hand, likely short in spades.
5. North's 2NT: Better than an average hand.
6. South's 3NT: Upper level of strength, 14 to 15 points.

What kind of hand does partner have? It's clear that partner does not have too many high-card points. His takeout double is primarily distributional. It must be in the unbid suits. Partner's takeout *Double* shouts as clearly as if he had bid, 2♣ and 2♥.

You are now in the position of leading partner's suit. As you have three hearts, your partnership should have more hearts than clubs. A heart lead is indicated.

With three small hearts, your system says, lead the top card.

The complete hand:

| Dealer: South | | | |
|---|---|---|---|
| | **North** | | |
| | ♠ A K 7 4 2 | | |
| | ♥ Q 4 | | |
| | ♦ Q 6 4 | | |
| | ♣ 10 4 3 | | |
| **West** | | **East** | |
| ♠ Q J 10 9 3 | | ♠ 8 | |
| ♥ 8 5 3 | | ♥ A J 10 9 2 | |
| ♦ J 10 9 | | ♦ 5 2 | |
| ♣ 6 5 | | ♣ A J 9 8 2 | |
| | **South** | | |
| | ♠ 6 5 | | |
| | ♥ K 7 6 | | |
| | ♦ A K 8 7 3 | | |
| | ♣ K Q 7 | | |

| Bidding: | West | North | East | South |
|---|---|---|---|---|
| | — | --- | --- | 1♦ |
| | Pass | 1♠ | Dbl. | 1NT |
| | Pass | 2NT | Pass | 3NT |
| | All Pass | | | |
| Opening Lead: ♥8 | | | | |

The heart lead establishes partner's suit. If dummy plays small, East plays the 9, permitting South to win. If dummy plays the queen, East plays the ace and continues the suit until South wins. South can run five diamonds and two spades, but must give up the lead to East in the club suit. Four hearts and one club defeat the contract.

Any lead, other than a heart, permits declarer to make the contract. A club trick can be cashed before the defense can establish the heart suit.

## RULE OF ELEVEN

When the long suits do not contain a sequence, the opening leads are often "fourth-best."

Why this standard procedure? Communication between defenders is a prime consideration in opening leads. The fourth-best lead permits partner to use the rule of eleven to help determine the location of outstanding cards.

Here's how the rule of eleven works:
When partner makes a fourth-best lead, subtract the number of that card from 11. The answer will tell you how many cards *higher* than the one led there are among the three other players.

These Examples will help clarify the principle.

| | |
|---|---|
| Example 1. | Dummy: ♦K 6 3 |
| Partner's lead: ♦7 | You: ♦A 10 9 2 |

Declarer has how many cards higher than the ♦7?

Subtract 7 from 11. That leaves four cards *higher* than the 7 among the dummy, you and declarer. You look at dummy and your own hand and make a simple calculation.

Dummy has one card higher and you have three higher cards. That leaves zero for the declarer. If dummy does not play the king, you can safely play the deuce on this trick. This allows partner to continue to lead the suit through the king.

```
Example 2.                 Dummy: ♦Q 9 3
   Partner's lead: ♦5                    You: ♦ K 10 7


Declarer has how many cards higher than the opening card
led?
```

|                    | 11                              |
| ------------------ | ------------------------------- |
| Subtract:          | -5                              |
| There are:         | 6 cards higher among the three players |
| Dummy and you have:| 5 cards higher.                 |
| Declarer has:      | 1 card higher.                  |

Assuming that declarer has an honor, you can safely play the
♦7 if dummy's 3♦ is played.. Declarer can obtain only one
trick on his combination of cards, whether his honor is the ace
or the jack.

   The rule of eleven is a two-edged sword. The declarer can use
the rule as well as the defenders. Defenders, however, need all the
help they can get.

♦ ♦ ♦ ♦ ♦

# DEFENSIVE PLAY

## *Third Hand Play*
## *Unblocking*

♦ ♦ ♦ ♦

## *Defensive Signaling*
## *Attitude*
## *Count*
## *Suit Preference*
## *Discarding*

♦ ♦ ♦ ♦

## *The Uppercut*

♦ ♦ ♦ ♦

## THIRD HAND PLAY

Defense is the area where partnership interdependence is most indicated. Whereas declarer always knows all his assets, a defender has only his half of the defense's resources in his view.

This has led to many clichés in advice given to defenders. "When in doubt lead trumps," "Play through strength, up to weakness," "Never finesse your partner," "Second hand low, third hand high," are among the bromides given to salve the anguish of puzzled defenders. Continuing in our cliché mold, all these pearls of wisdom should be taken with a grain of salt.

We will concentrate on Third Hand Play.
"Third hand high" is a relative term. It should really say, "The most *effective* high card." And we can add to that, "The most *informative* high card." Defensive play must *communicate* with your partner, as well as being effective.

| Example: | *Dummy* |
|----------|---------|
|          | ♦ Q 10 7 |

| *Partner's Lead* | *You* |
|------------------|-------|
| ♦ 2              | ♦ K J 9 4 |

In relation to dummy's holding your cards are "equals." Your most effective play depends upon which card is played by dummy. If the ♦7 is played you'd play the ♦9; if the ♦10, your ♦J; if the ♦Q, your ♦K. We can modify the cliché to read, "The *lowest* effective *high* card."

We all know that when leading, we play the *top* of a sequence. It helps partner realize that you most likely have the adjacent lower cards as well. When you independently lead a queen, partner can reasonably assume that you have Q J 10 or Q J 9.

Why then do we recommend that in third hand we play the *bottom* of touching cards?

Consider this scenario: The opponents have reached a 3NT contract.

```
                        Dummy
                        ♠ 6 5
                        ♥ Q 8 4
                        ♦ Q 6 2
                        ♣ K Q J 8 7 2


You
♠ K 10 8 3
♥ 10 7 6 5
♦ 10 9 8
♣ A 5
```

Your opening lead: ♠3

Partner plays the ♠Q which is won by declarer's ♠A. Declarer plays the ♣10. You hold off and win the second round with your ace. You would like to continue spades, but are afraid to because it might set up declarer's ♠J.

You try to reach partner in another suit, so he can play spades through declarer. Diamonds seems as good a bet as any. You play the ♦10. Dummy's queen wins and declarer runs four diamonds and the club suit for a total of nine tricks.

Change the scenario slightly:

On your opening spade lead partner plays the ♠J which is won by declarer's ♠A. Declarer starts on clubs and you win the second round. This time you *know* partner has the ♠Q. (If declarer had it he would have won the first trick with the queen, not the ace.)

You can safely underlead your ♠K 10 to partner's ♠Q. Partner can return the suit and you wind up with three spade tricks.

This is the complete hand:

**Dummy**
North
♠ 6 5
♥ Q 8 4
♦ Q 6
♣ K Q J 8 7 2

**You**
West
♠ K 10 8 3
♥ 10 7 6 5
♦ 10 9 8
♣ A 5

**Partner**
East
♠ Q J 2
♥ A 9 3 2
♦ 7 5 3 2
♣ 4 3

**Declarer**
South
♠ A 9 7 4
♥ K J
♦ A K J 4
♣ 10 9 6

You readily can see what a great difference it makes to you if partner correctly plays the ♠J rather than the incorrect ♠Q.

Now partner is on lead with the ♠Q. He can return a spade and then on your fourth spade signal with the ♥9, requesting a heart return to his ace for the setting trick. Better yet, he cashes the ♥A first, before returning the spade, not giving partner a chance to go wrong. Never ask your partner to do something that you can do yourself.

In defense, helping partner is the name of the game, *the winning game.* . .

## UNBLOCKING

OUTA THE WAY, PARTNER, WE'RE COMING THROUGH!

GET THE **BIG FELLOW** OUT OF THE WAY!

In defense, the most horrible specter presented to the new player is "trumping your partner's ace." Most of the times it is a terrible blunder (but every once in a while it is the correct play). This type of fear, of appearing to make an egregious error, extends to overtaking partner's high honor with your high honor. But quite *often* it is the correct play.

Here are a few examples:

Opponents are in a 3NT contract.

```
                    Dummy
                    ♥ 7 6
    Partner                          You
    ♥ K Q J 9 4 2                    ♥ A 3
                    Declarer
                    ♥ 10 8 5
```

Partner's Opening Lead: ♥K

In this situation it is essential that you overtake partner's king with your ace. Failure to make this "unblocking play" may very well hand the contract to the declarer. You would be forced to win the second trick with your ace. Having no more hearts, you'd have to play another suit. Declarer could likely run off his nine tricks before partner could regain the lead

|  | *Dummy* |  |
|---|---|---|
|  | ♠ 9 4 |  |
| *Partner* |  | *You* |
| ♠ Q J 10 8 7 3 |  | ♠ K 5 |
|  | *Declarer* |  |
|  | ♠ A 6 2 |  |

Against a 3NT contract partner's opening lead is: ♠Q

Here again, it is necessary to overtake partner's queen with your king. If declarer holds up the ace, you can continue the suit by playing the ♠5. Declarer may hold up again, but partner is now in the lead with the ♠10 and can continue playing the suit. Declarer is forced to play the ace. Eventually, with one outside entry, partner can run the suit.

Let's look at the complete hand:

*Dummy*
North
♠ 9 4
♥ A J 10
♦ K 10 9 6
♣ Q 10 4 2

*Partner*
West
♠ Q J 10 8 7 3
♥ K 5
♦ A 7 2
♣ 8 5

*You*
East
♠ K 5
♥ 9 7 6 3 2
♦ 8 5
♣ 9 7 6 3

*Declarer*
South
♠ A 6 2
♥ Q 8 4
♦ Q J 4 3
♣ A K J

Notice what would have happened if you had not unblocked your king. If declarer holds up his ace, your king would be forced to win the second round. As you are unable to continue the suit, declarer still retains his ace as a stopper. When partner regains the lead with the ♦A, he is not able to run the spade suit. Instead of being set, declarer makes an overtrick.

♦ ♦ ♦ ♦

The unblocking principle works in suit contracts as well as in notrump contracts.

The opponents reach a 4♠ contract via a simple auction. Your partner's opening lead is the ♦K.

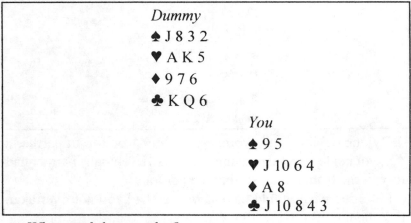

*Dummy*
♠ J 8 3 2
♥ A K 5
♦ 9 7 6
♣ K Q 6

*You*
♠ 9 5
♥ J 10 6 4
♦ A 8
♣ J 10 8 4 3

What card do you play?

If you correctly play the ace, and return the suit, partner will win the second trick. On the third round of the suit, partner will play a winning high diamond or a small one which you will ruff. If partner can produce another trick later on, you will set the contract.

The complete hand:

```
                    Dummy
                    North
                    ♠ J 8 3 2
                    ♥ A K 5
                    ♦ 9 7 6
                    ♣ K Q 6
  Partner                           You
  West                              East
  ♠ K 4                             ♠ 9 5
  ♥ 8 3 2                           ♥ J 10 6 4
  ♦ K Q 10 4 3                      ♦ A 8
  ♣ 9 5 2                           ♣ J 10 8 4 3
                    Declarer
                    South
                    ♠ A Q 10 7 6
                    ♥ Q 9 7
                    ♦ J 5 2
                    ♣ A 7
```

By unblocking, when you played the ♦A on top of partner's ♦K, your side won three diamond tricks. Eventually partner had to win the trump king, setting the contract.

Let's see what would have happened had you not overtaken the opening lead with your ♦A.

Partner's diamond continuation would have forced you to win with your ace. Your best return would be a small trump. Declarer, however, should refuse to finesse and hop up with the ace. Playing three rounds of clubs, ending in dummy, enables declarer to discard his losing diamond. He now gives up a trick to the ♠K, making his contract, losing only *two diamonds* and one trump.

Your unblocking play has successfully blocked declarer from making his contract.

## DEFENSIVE SIGNALING

With you not seeing partner's cards and he not seeing yours, communication between the defenders is a real problem. As a result, legal signaling systems have been devised to help alleviate the situation.

The system we will discuss here is considered standard. Were you to sit down to play with a first-time partner and have no prior discussion, these are the methods you can expect to use.

There are three basic areas covered in the signaling system:
1. Attitude: "I like!" or "I don't like!"
2. Count: "I have an odd number of cards in the suit." or
        "I have an even number of cards in the suit."
3. Suit Preference: Signaling in a third suit to show preference between two other suits.

### ATTITUDE

Partner leads a suit. You may want him to continue to play that suit or not.

If you would like him to continue, play the *highest* card you can afford. If he then plays a card in that suit that retains the lead, you follow with your lowest card. This "High-Low" is a come on. It asks partner to continue the suit.

If you would like him to discontinue, play your *lowest* card *first*, then the next higher card.

Note: When defending a trump contract, and partner leads the ace from AK or the king from AK (depending on your style), do not high-low with a queen-doubleton (Qx) unless the hand also contains the jack (Q J). Playing the queen first implies that it is

215

a singleton or that you also have the jack. Partner can then safely underlead the high honor, knowing that you can win the trick with the jack or ruff it if the queen was a singleton.

You can also indicate attitude when discarding. If opponents are playing a suit in which you are void, you can discard high-low in a suit in which you are interested or low-high in a suit in which you have no interest.

Sometimes you cannot afford a high card in a suit when discarding. Inferentially, you indicate strength in *that* suit by discarding low cards in the *other* suits.

Let's take a look at this hand.

| You are East and the bidding has gone: | | | |
| North | East | South | West |
| — | — | 1 ♥ | 1 ♠ |
| 2 ♥ | Pass | 3 ♥ | Pass |
| 4 ♥ | All Pass | | |

Partner leads ♠A (Ace from Ace-King)

*Dummy*
North
♠ Q 7 4
♥ Q 10 9 7
♦ A 9 5 4
♣ 7 6

*You*
East
♠ 8 3
♥ 8 6 5
♦ J 8 2
♣ Q J 9 5 2

What card do you play?

Although you see the ♠Q in dummy, you'd like partner to continue because you have a doubleton and can ruff the third round of the suit. You play the ♠8, asking partner to continue. Partner dutifully follows your direction and you ruff the third round of spades.

Eventually, your side must win a diamond trick to set the contract. The high-low signal was the catalyst that provided the ruff to defeat the contract.

The complete hand:

```
                        Dummy
                        North
                        ♠ Q 7 4
                        ♥ Q 10 9 7
                        ♦ A 9 5 4
                        ♣ 7 6

        Partner                         You
        West                            East
        ♠ A K 10 6 2                    ♠ 8 3
        ♥ 4                             ♥ 8 6 5
        ♦ K Q 6 3                       ♦ J 8 2
        ♣ 10 8 4                        ♣ Q J 9 5 2

                        Declarer
                        South
                        ♠ J 9 5
                        ♥ A K J 3 2
                        ♦ 10 7
                        ♣ A K 3
```

Now let's look at a slightly different situation. The bidding and the contract are the same. South is the declarer in a 4♥ contract.

What do we do in this case?

Partner leads ♠A (Ace from Ace-King)

*Dummy*
North
♠ Q 7 4
♥ Q 10 9 7
♦ A 9 5 4
♣ 7 6

*You*
East
♠ 8 5 3
♥ 8 6 5
♦ J 8 2
♣ Q J 9 5

What card do you play?

You must play the ♠3. "Partner, do not continue playing spades. You will be setting up dummy's queen for a possible discard of a loser. Switch to another suit!" If partner is paying attention, and he should, he will do just that.

He switches to the ♦K. You like the lead and indicate that by playing the ♦8.

The complete hand:

```
                        Dummy
                        North
                        ♠ Q 7 4
                        ♥ Q 10 9 7
                        ♦ A 9 5 4
                        ♣ 7 6
        Partner                         You
        West                            East
        ♠ A K 10 6 2                    ♠ 8 5 3
        ♥ 4                             ♥ 8 6 5
        ♦ K Q 6                         ♦ J 8 2
        ♣ 10 8 4 2                      ♣ Q J 9 5
                        Declarer
                        South
                        ♠ J 9
                        ♥ A K J 3 2
                        ♦ 10 7 3
                        ♣ A K 3
```

Declarer wins the ♦A in dummy, draws trumps and plays a spade towards the queen. But partner hops up with the ♠K and switches to the ♦Q, on which you play the deuce. This now completes your high-low echo and partner continues a diamond to your jack, which sets the contract.

Notice what a significant role the "simple" attitude signals played in defeating both contracts. The go-ahead signal in the first hand enabled partner to give you the ruff to set the contract. The discontinue signal in the second hand permitted partner to switch to the diamond suit to set up winners before declarer could utilize the ♠Q for a discard.

There was no way partner could have had the knowledge to make the right decisions without your help with the attitude signals.

HOLDING AN EVEN NUMBER OF CARDS IN A SUIT, PLAY: **HIGH-LOW** | HOLDING AN ODD NUMBER OF CARDS IN A SUIT, PLAY: **LOW-HIGH**

It is often important for partner to know how many cards you have in a suit. You play high-low in a suit where you hold an even number of cards, (2,4,6) and up-the-line starting with your lowest card when you hold an odd number of cards (1,3,5).

This is particularly true when the opponents are playing a suit. You may want to know when it is advantageous to win a trick.

Let's look at this 3NT contract by South. (Playing 16-18 notrumps they arrived at the contract with a simple 1NT-2NT-3NT auction.)

Partner's opening lead is: ♠J

|  |
|---|
| *Dummy* |
| North |
| ♠ Q 6 5 |
| ♥ 6 5 |
| ♦ K Q J 5 3 |
| ♣ 8 7 5 |
| *You* |
| East |
| ♠ K 8 2 |
| ♥ Q 9 3 2 |
| ♦ A 6 4 |
| ♣ J 9 2 |

Dummy plays small and you play an encouraging ♠8 and declarer wins the trick with the ♠A. Declarer now plays the ♦10. As South had opened 1NT you know he has at least two diamonds in his hand so you surely are not going to win the first play of the suit. But do you win the second or hold up to the third round? It all depends on which cards partner plays.

On the first round partner plays the ♦7 and you follow with your ♦4. You are still in the dark. On the next trick declarer leads the ♦2 and partner plays the ♦8. The moment of truth has arrived. Do you win the trick or hold up for another round?

Partner's ♦7 initially was a fairly high card but his next play, the ♦8 was higher, so he must hold three diamonds. Declarer originally held only two diamonds You must win the second trick.

The complete hand:

|  | Dummy | |
| --- | --- | --- |
|  | North | |
|  | ♠ Q 6 5 | |
|  | ♥ 6 5 | |
|  | ♦ K Q J 5 3 | |
|  | ♣ 8 7 5 | |
| Partner | | You |
| West | | East |
| ♠ J 10 9 3 | | ♠ K 8 2 |
| ♥ K 10 7 4 | | ♥ Q 9 3 2 |
| ♦ 9 8 7 | | ♦ A 6 4 |
| ♣ 10 4 | | ♣ J 9 2. |
|  | Declarer | |
|  | South | |
|  | ♠ A 7 4 | |
|  | ♥ A J 8 | |
|  | ♦ 10 2 | |
|  | ♣ A K Q 6 3 | |

Contract: 3NT by South
Opening lead: ♠J

221

If you allow declarer to win the second diamond trick he will stop playing the suit and cash five clubs and the ♥A. This adds up to the nine tricks he needs for his contract.

How can you tell the difference between count signals and attitude signals? Attitude signals are given when partner leads a suit. Count signals are given when the opponents play a suit. Do you always give count signals? Only when it will help your side more than declarer's.

(A little sidelight is the count signal in the trump suit. It is just the opposite of the regular suit count. You high-low with three cards and play low-high with two. The purpose is to indicate to partner that you may have a third trump available for ruffing purposes. Again do this only if it can help your side more than the declarer.)

## SUIT PREFERENCE

It's often desirable to direct partner to lead a specific suit when he obtains the lead. The gadget that makes this possible is the *Suit Preference Signal*. Here's how it works. Partner may have a choice of two suits to lead. You indicate your preference between the two suits by signaling in a third suit. Play the highest card you can spare in the third suit for the higher ranking suit, play your lowest card for the lower ranking suit.

A handy use of the suit preference signal is when you are giving partner a card to ruff and you want to tell him which suit to return.

Against a 4♠ contract by South, you've gotten off to a great lead, the ♦A.

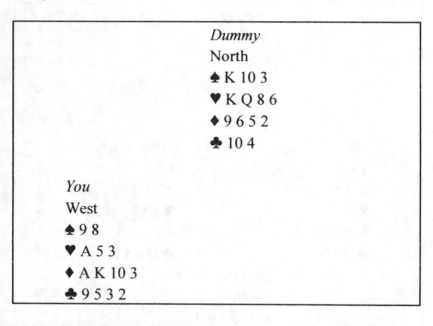

*Dummy*
North
♠ K 10 3
♥ K Q 8 6
♦ 9 6 5 2
♣ 10 4

*You*
West
♠ 9 8
♥ A 5 3
♦ A K 10 3
♣ 9 5 3 2

After the ace holds you continue the king and partner discards a club. You know that after partner ruffs the next diamond you can give him a second ruff *if you can tell him which suit to play back to you.* With the suit preference signal you can.

The two outstanding suits other than trumps are hearts and clubs. Return the ♦10 if you want hearts (the higher ranking suit) or the ♦3 if you want clubs (the lower ranking suit).

In this case you hold the ♥A, so you return the ♦10. Partner dutifully obeys. You play another diamond for him to ruff and the contract is set two tricks.

If left to his own devices, it would be very unlikely that he would return a heart with dummy's ♥ K Q staring him in the face.

223

The complete hand:

Dummy
North
♠ K 10 3
♥ K Q 8 6
♦ 9 6 5 2
♣ 10 4

You
West
♠ 9 8
♥ A 5 3
♦ A K 10 3
♣ 9 5 3 2

Partner
East
♠ 7 5 2
♥ 10 9 7 4 2
♦ 8
♣ Q J 8 6

Declarer
South
♠ A Q J 6 4
♥ J
♦ Q J 7 4
♣ A K 7

Contract: 4♠ by South. Opening lead: ♦A

Here's another example of how the Suit Preference Signal can come into play.

The bidding:

| North | East | South | West |
|-------|------|-------|------|
| —     | —    | —     | 1♥   |
| 1NT   | 2♥   | 4♠    | All Pass |

You are West and lead the ♥A.

Dummy comes down and this is what you see:

*Dummy*
North
♠ A J 6
♥ K Q 7
♦ K 8 7
♣ K 8 7 6

*You*
♠ K 2
♥ A 10 6 4 2
♦ Q 10 9
♣ Q J 10

Oops! Maybe you should not have led the ♥A. But partner did support you. Oh, well, the fat is in the fire. What do you do now? It is obvious that you cannot continue hearts. Declarer will get immediate discards of losers on the ♥ K Q. Do you switch to the ♦Q or ♣Q? Maybe partner can help.

*Partner:* East
♠ 4 3
♥ J 9 8 3
♦ A J 6 5
♣ 9 5 3

Using the suit preference signal partner has to *shout,* "Switch to diamonds!" He plays the ♥J, telling you to play diamonds, the higher ranking of the two relevant suits. The ♥J could not be misread as an attitude signal. The ♥9 might have been. The diamond play garners the three tricks needed to set the contract.

To complete the picture here is declarer's hand:

South
♠ Q 10 9 8 7 5
♥ 5
♦ 4 3 2
♣ A 4 2

## ATTITUDE DISCARDS

In addition to attitude signals in response to partner's leads, you also are able to indicate an interest or lack of interest in a suit when discarding.

Play a high card you can spare in a suit you like (followed by the lowest card if you continue to discard in that suit).

To show lack of interest in a suit play your lowest card (followed by your next lowest on your next discard in that suit).

Example:

> You are West and are on lead after hearing this auction:
>
> | West | North | East | South |
> |------|-------|------|-------|
> | — | Pass | Pass | 1 NT |
> | Pass | 2♣ | Pass | 2♦ |
> | Pass | 3 NT | All Pass | |
>
> *Dummy*
> ♠ K J 7 3
> ♥ K J 6 5
> ♦ J 6
> ♣ Q 10 2
>
> *You*
> ♠ 10 8 4
> ♥ A 8 4 2
> ♦ K Q 10 9 4
> ♣ 4

You lead the ♦K. You see dummy and continue the ♦Q and ♦9 as declarer holds up and wins with the ♦A. Partner follows to the three rounds and dummy discards the ♣2.

A club is led to dummy's queen which holds the trick. The ♣10 is played. What card do you play at your turn? Yes, you're right. The ♥8. Regardless of what card partner had played, you must show him that your entry is in hearts.

The complete hand:

| | Dummy | |
| --- | --- | --- |
| | North | |
| | ♠ K J 7 3 | |
| | ♥ K J 6 5 | |
| | ♦ J 6 | |
| | ♣ Q 10 2 | |

| You | | Partner |
| --- | --- | --- |
| West | | East |
| ♠ 10 8 4 | | ♠ 9 6 2 |
| ♥ A 8 4 2 | | ♥ 10 9 3 |
| ♦ K Q 10 9 4 | | ♦ 8 7 2 |
| ♣ 4 | Declarer | ♣ A 7 5 3 |

| | South | |
| --- | --- | --- |
| | ♠ A Q 5 | |
| | ♥ Q 7 | |
| | ♦ A 5 3 | |
| | ♣ K J 9 8 6 | |

Partner may have held up winning the ♣A to give you a chance to signal a way to reach your hand, which you dutifully did. Can you imagine partner staring at dummy's ♠ KJ73 ♥ KJ65 and trying to figure out which suit to lead to you, without your help?

Partnership communication takes two to tango. One to signal and the other to watch and heed its message.

Let's look at another scenario.

You are West and the bidding has gone:

| West | North | East | South |
| --- | --- | --- | --- |
| — | — | — | 1♥ |
| Pass | 3♥* | Pass | 4♥ |
| All Pass | * Forcing raise | | |

The contract is 4♥ by South and partner leads: ♣J

**Dummy**
♠ K 9 7
♥ J 7 6 2          *You*
♦ K 9 7          ♠ 8 6 4 3 2
♣ A K 2          ♥ 5
                 ♦ A J 10 2
                 ♣ 8 6 3

Dummy wins the club lead. Trumps are led to declarer's ♥AK and you now have to discard. What card do you play? If partner should gain the lead, you'd like him to play a diamond. You can't afford to discard the ♦J or ♦10, it could easily sacrifice a trick. In this case you have to create a negative inference by playing your lowest spade. You're saying, "Partner don't play spades if you obtain the lead."

Here's the complete hand and see where we go from there

**Dummy**
♠ K 9 7
♥ J 7 6 2
♦ K 9 7
♣ A K 2

*Partner*                          *You*
♠ Q 10 5                          ♠ 8 6 4 3 2
♥ Q 9 3                           ♥ 5
♦ Q 8 4                           ♦ A J 10 2
♣ J 10 9 5                        ♣ 8 6 3

**Declarer**
♠ A J
♥ A K 10 8 4
♦ 6 5 3
♣ Q 7 4

When declarer discovers the bad trump break he clears the club suit and exits with a trump to partner's queen on which you now discard your second lowest spade. By this time partner should have gotten your message, "Don't play spades, play a diamond!"

The most effective lead is the ♦Q. It retains the lead if dummy does not cover. It rolls in three diamond tricks, which in addition to the trump trick sets the contract.

This is just the tip of the iceberg in the possibilities of defensive attitude signaling. When you can't afford positive signals, try to use negative inferences. The results will always depend upon both partners being on the same wavelength and paying close attention to all the "little" cards that are played.

♦ ♦ ♦ ♦

Every once in a while you have the opportunity to utilize a presumably useless small trump to set up a trick for your partner. This defensive maneuver is delightfully nicknamed, *The Uppercut*. Here is an example:

The opponents are in a 4♥ contract. Partner leads the ♠A. Dummy comes down and this is what you see:

|                | *Dummy*    |
|----------------|------------|
|                | ♠ Q 7 5    |
|                | ♥ A 9 8    |
|                | ♦ 8 7 5 4  |
|                | ♣ Q J 10   |
|                | *You*      |
|                | ♠ 9 2      |
|                | ♥ 7 2      |
|                | ♦ A 10 9 2 |
|                | ♣ 8 6 5 3 2 |

On partner's ♠A lead followed by the ♠K you high-low with your ♠9 and 2. A third spade is led to dummy's queen.

Here's your chance to be a hero. *Give 'em the uppercut!*
Trump with the ♥7 (not the deuce)! Let's see what happens.

The Complete Hand:

```
                    Dummy
                    ♠ Q 7 5
                    ♥ A 9 8
                    ♦ 8 7 5 4
                    ♣ Q J 10
Partner                             You
♠ A K J 10 8 3                      ♠ 9 2
♥ J 10 3                            ♥ 7 2
♦ 6 3                               ♦ A 10 9 2
♣ 9 7                               ♣ 8 6 5 3 2
                    Declarer
                    ♠ 6 4
                    ♥ K Q 6 5 4
                    ♦ K Q J
                    ♣ A K 4
```

Contract: 4♥ by South
Opening lead: ♠A

Your ♥7 forces declarer to overtrump with the ♥Q. This
establishes a sure trump trick for you partner's ♥ J 10 3 holding.
As declarer has no way of avoiding a diamond loser, the
uppercut with the measly little trump seven defeats an otherwise
sound contract.

Note what would have happened if you had incorrectly ruffed
with the deuce. Declarer would have overtrumped with the ♥4,
drawn trumps, surrendered a diamond trick and made his
contract.

Keep on the lookout for the uppercut. It comes up in actual play more often than you may think. Occasionally it is even correct to ruff partner's "winning" high card in order to force a high trump from declarer.

As an example, let's swap a couple of cards. Give the ♠Q to partner and the ♠J to dummy. Now when partner plays the ♠Q on the third play of the suit it is still necessary to ruff with the ♥7 to defeat the contract.

In order to give his partner less of a problem, a perceptive defender aware of his own trump holding, might have underled his ♠Q to force partner to ruff the trick. And, of course, ruffing with ♥7, not the deuce, is the correct play.

## WRAP-UP

At this point, many essential areas of declarer and defender play have been covered. As you expand your bridge playing experience, you undoubtedly will be exposed to many more aspects and nuances of this wonderful game.

Executing a triple squeeze by rectifying the count doesn't come up that often! Nor do sophisticated maneuvers such as a Deschapelles or Merrimack coup. They're tough enough to pronounce and spell, let alone recognize the opportunity to use them.

But, getting stuck in the wrong hand, taking the wrong finesse, developing suits in the wrong order, leading the wrong card, they happen all the time. Just observe the play around you. These are the areas that bring the downfall of even "experienced" players.

Review the various chapters from time to time. They will refresh your awareness of the important tactics that occur at the bridge table every day.

Pay heed to the bidding. It will pay dividends in both declarer and defensive play. Above all, maintain a pleasant but serious attitude towards the game. It will result in better card play for fun and fortune.

### A final friendly thought.

When speaking with my social bridge playing friends I am often asked this question. "What can I do to become a better bridge player?" Perhaps this may help. Let me leave you with this thought.

The answer is both "simple"and important. Every time you are dealt a hand go through a simple ritual:

    1. Count your cards face down.

    2. Sort the cards into suits.

    3. Before counting your points, *count your distribution.*

*Say to yourself,* "I have a 5-5-2-1 hand." or "a 4-4-4-1 hand." or "5-3-3-2 hand." You become aware of hand patterns. Occasionally you may say, "I have a 5-4-2-1 hand—*oops!*---that's only 12 cards." You'll then fiddle with your fingers and perhaps find that missing ace and you will go on from there. You'll never have to say, "I'm sorry, I would have bid but the ace of diamonds was hidden."

The main idea is that you focus on hand patterns. After you know about your own hand, you can then concentrate on the other players at the table, both opponents and your partner.

If an opponent makes an opening bid of 1♠, his partner responds 1 NT and opener rebids 2♥, you now have a pretty good picture of his hand. He holds at least five spades and four hearts. That leaves room for only four cards in the minor suits.

Being aware of hand patterns puts you on the road to the ability to "count the hand." As an example, if you are a defender and you have an idea of declarer's distribution, when dummy comes down you can surmise partner's distribution as well.

Experienced players have a delightful way of describing a hand. Counting down in the order of spades, hearts, diamonds and clubs, they say, "I had a fifty-five, twenty-one hand," to describe a hand containing five spades, five hearts, two diamonds and a club. "Forty-one, forty-four" and "Fifteen, forty-three," describe four spades, one heart and four diamonds and four clubs in the first hand and one spade, five hearts, four diamonds and three clubs in the second hand.

Invest the effort to make this procedure a part of your routine. It will pay dividends for a lifetime of better bridge.

The fat is in the fire. Take it from here.

♦ ♦ ♦ ♦

# ACKNOWLEDGMENTS

Bridge books just don't happen by themselves. People and organizations play a role, not merely in the short term but in the long run as well.

Gerry Gerstenberg put her computer know-how to good use in the difficult task of bridge typesetting. Thank you, Gerry.

Sid Stone did careful reading of the manuscript to hopefully keep bugs out of the final copy. Thank you, Sid.

And my special thanks to Randy Baron for your confidence and support of my *Fun Way* bridge books. Your counsel and advice helped make writing this book a joy.

The two bridge organizations, most important to me, must not go unmentioned.

**The American Contract Bridge League** cannot be taken for granted. For more than 60 years it enabled me to enjoy this wonderful game from my teenage years until today. Even in my army days I played in the USO clubs. Over the years ACBL provided the on-the-job training plus pleasurable experiences in its club games and tournaments.

**The American Bridge Teachers' Association** is the second influential organization in my life. In 1976, upon retiring from the business world, I decided to teach this wonderful game. I felt I had to accomplish two things if I were to be entitled to call myself a bridge teacher. The first was to become a Life Master. I rushed to obtain the various color points needed. The second was to become a certified teacher of the ABTA. I started teaching and drawing cartoon charts to help put ideas across. I attended my first ABTA convention in Chicago in 1977. The 25 years of participation in ABTA helped hone my skills as a teacher. The interaction among the members cross-pollinated our experiences and made us all better teachers.

# 50 HIGHLY-RECOMMENDED TITLES

**CALL TOLL FREE 1-800-274-2221
IN THE U.S. & CANADA TO ORDER ANY OF
THEM OR TO REQUEST OUR
FULL-COLOR 64 PAGE CATALOG OF
ALL BRIDGE BOOKS IN PRINT,
SUPPLIES AND GIFTS.**

## FOR BEGINNERS
#0300 Future Champions' Bridge Series ................................. 9.95
#2130 Kantar-Introduction to Declarer's Play ...................... 10.00
#2135 Kantar-Introduction to Defender's Play ..................... 10.00
#0101 Stewart-Baron-The Bridge Book 1 .............................. 9.95
#1121 Silverman-Elementary Bridge
       Five Card Major Student Text ................................... 4.95
#0660 Penick-Beginning Bridge Complete ........................... 9.95
#0661 Penick-Beginning Bridge Quizzes ............................. 6.95
#3230 Lampert-Fun Way to Serious Bridge ........................ 10.00

## FOR ADVANCED PLAYERS
#2250 Reese-Master Play ............................................... 5.95
#1420 Klinger-Modern Losing Trick Count .......................... 12.95
#2240 Love-Bridge Squeezes Complete ............................. 7.95
#0103 Stewart-Baron-The Bridge Book 3 ............................ 9.95
#0740 Woolsey-Matchpoints ......................................... 14.95
#0741 Woolsey-Partnership Defense ................................. 12.95
#1702 Bergen-Competitive Auctions .................................. 11.95

## BIDDING — 2 OVER 1 GAME FORCE
#4750 Bruno & Hardy-Two-Over-One Game Force:
       An Introduction ................................................. 9.95
#1750 Hardy-Two-Over-One Game Force ........................... 14.95
#1790 Lawrence-Workbook on the Two Over One System 12.95
#4525 Lawrence-Bidding Quizzes Book 1 ........................... 13.95

Prices subject to change without notice.

## DEFENSE
#0520 Blackwood-Complete Book of Opening Leads........... 17.95
#0104 Stewart-Baron-The Bridge Book 4 .............................. 7.95
#0631 Lawrence-Dynamic Defense ......................................... 11.95
#1200 Woolsey-Modern Defensive Signalling ........................ 4.95


## FOR INTERMEDIATE PLAYERS
#3015 Root-Commonsense Bidding ....................................... 15.00
#0630 Lawrence-Card Combinations ..................................... 12.95
#0102 Stewart-Baron-The Bridge Book 2 .............................. 9.95
#1122 Silverman-Intermediate Bridge Five
       Card Major Student Text ...................................... 4.95
#0575 Lampert-The Fun Way to Advanced Bridge ............. 11.95
#0633 Lawrence-How to Read Your Opponents' Cards ....... 11.95
#3672 Truscott-Bid Better, Play Better ................................. 12.95
#1765 Lawrence-Judgment at Bridge ................................... 11.95

## PLAY OF THE HAND
#2150 Kantar-Test your Bridge Play, Vol. 1 ....................... 10.00
#3675 Watson-Watson's Classic Book on
       the Play of the Hand .............................................. 16.00
#1932 Mollo-Gardener-Card Play Technique ........................ 19.95
#3009 Root-How to Play a Bridge Hand ............................. 16.00
#1124 Silverman-Play of the Hand as
       Declarer and Defender ........................................... 4.95
#2175 Truscott-Winning Declarer Play ................................. 10.00
#3803 Sydnor-Bridge Made Easy Book 3 ............................. 8.00

## CONVENTIONS
#2115 Kantar-Bridge Conventions ......................................... 10.00
#0610 Kearse-Bridge Conventions Complete ....................... 29.95
#3011 Root-Pavlicek-Modern Bridge Conventions ................. 15.00
#0240 Championship Bridge Series (All 36) ........................ 25.95

## DUPLICATE STRATEGY
#1600 Klinger-50 Winning Duplicate Tips ............................ 14.95
#2260 Sheinwold-Duplicate Bridge ....................................... 4.95
#2800 Granovetter-Conventions at a Glance ........................ 8.95
#1750 Hardy-2 Over 1 Game Force ..................................... 14.95
#2038 Seagram-25 Bridge Conventions You Should Know ...... 15.95

## FOR ALL PLAYERS
#3889 Darvas & de V. Hart-Right Through The Pack ......... 14.95
#0790 Simon- Why You Lose at Bridge ............................... 11.95
#1928 Mollo- Bridge in the Menagerie ................................. 16.95

## DEVYN PRESS INC.

3600 Chamberlain Lane, Suite 230, Louisville, KY 40241

### 1-800-274-2221

CALL TOLL FREE IN THE U.S. & CANADA
TO ORDER OR TO REQUEST OUR 64 PAGE
FULL COLOR CATALOG OF BRIDGE BOOKS,
SUPPLIES AND GIFTS.